Healing Spirits

Star of the popular ITV series *Star Psychic* and showbiz medium *du jour*, Sally Morgan is the country's most accurate and respected psychic. Her memoir, *My Psychic Life*, was a *Sunday Times* top ten bestseller.

Healing Spirits

SALLY MORGAN

PENGUIN BOOKS

PENGUIN BOOKS

Published by the Penguin Group
Penguin Books Ltd, 80 Strand, London WC2R ORL, England
Penguin Group (USA) Inc., 375 Hudson Street, New York, New York 10014, USA
Penguin Group (Canada), 90 Eglinton Avenue East, Suite 700, Toronto, Ontario, Canada M4P 2Y3
(a division of Pearson Penguin Canada Inc.)
Penguin Ireland, 25 St Stephen's Green, Dublin 2, Ireland (a division of Penguin Books Ltd)
Penguin Group (Australia), 250 Camberwell Road, Camberwell, Victoria 3124, Australia
(a division of Pearson Australia Group Pty Ltd)
Penguin Books India Pvt Ltd, 11 Community Centre, Panchsheel Park, New Delhi – 110 017, India
Penguin Group (NZ), 67 Apollo Drive, Rosedale, North Shore 0632, New Zealand
(a division of Pearson New Zealand Ltd)
Penguin Books (South Africa) (Pty) Ltd, 24 Sturdee Avenue,
Rosebank, Johannesburg 2196, South Africa

Penguin Books Ltd, Registered Offices: 80 Strand, London WC2R ORL, England

www.penguin.com

First published 2009
2

Copyright © Sally Morgan, 2009
All rights reserved

The moral right of the author has been asserted

Set in Monotype Garamond
Typeset by Rowland Phototypesetting Ltd, Bury St Edmunds, Suffolk
Printed in England by Clays Ltd, St Ives plc

ISBN: 978-0-141-04354-8

www.greenpenguin.co.uk

Acknowledgements

To spirit world for a lifetime of knowledge.

To Unc-Unc and Rita for a lifetime of love.

To Yvonne and Christine for a lifetime of friendship.

Thank you all – especially Andrew, whose help, guidance and patience show me the way.

Not forgetting Penguin, thank you for allowing me to put my thoughts and spiritual adventures on paper. I am for ever grateful.

One

'You're one of those, aren't you?' she said. 'One of those people who see things?' Her name was Pat, an Irish nurse who worked on the same ward as I did. She was a lovely woman, a brilliant nurse.

I was twenty-eight and working at the South London Hospital for Women, a very old hospital. It's no longer there, replaced by flats now, I think – but it had started life as what they called a lying-in hospital. They don't have them these days, of course, but back in the 1800s when you had a baby you stayed in hospital for ten days, which was your 'lying-in' period. Can you believe that? Nowadays, they turf you out five minutes after you've given birth. Then, you had almost two weeks in which to recover from your ordeal and you did it in a women-only environment, in these huge, cavernous, Victorian wards lined with steel beds; stern-looking matrons clip-clopping up and down dispensing rebukes – quietness was insisted upon – plus maybe the odd spoonful of castor oil here and there.

By 1979, it was different. There was no lying-in any more. No longer was the ward used to help ease new life into the world. Now, it was part of the oncology unit and women came here to live out their last moments, before they were taken by the cancer. It was still quiet on the ward, but for a different reason. Death has the effect of cloaking a place with stillness.

And it was quiet that day, too, as I arrived for my shift, taking over from Pat. I walked through the ward towards the nurses' station at the far end. There, a curtain was drawn around one of the beds, and as I passed I suddenly had one of my knowings – that's what I call them, my 'knowings' – and I realized I knew almost all there was to know about the person behind the curtain. I knew it was a woman, of course, but I found I had a sense of what she looked like, and of her name. Most of all I knew that she was close –

Oh, really, very close. She had moments to live.

I'd not long been working on the oncology ward. Because of my ability I'd always had what you might call a close relationship with death; it didn't scare me. I'd never seen anybody die before, though. Not right before my eyes.

I came to a halt in front of Pat, who looked up, a greeting on her lips, about to hand me the nurse's report, which keeps you abreast of all that's going on in the ward. I didn't need to read the nurse's report for this particular woman, though, I knew just what Pat would say, that . . .

'She's about to die,' I said to Pat, indicating the curtain.

She looked at me sharply, eyes narrowing. 'How do you know?'

I always used to feel a certain way in those circumstances. A pride in my ability, plus a little embarrassment – a sort of social embarrassment, I suppose. I don't feel it much any more, of course. But I used to, back then. I used to get it a lot.

'I just do,' I said (yes, feeling that familiar pride-embarrassment twinge), 'I just know.'

Which is when she said, 'You're one of those, aren't you ... ?'

'Yes,' I replied, 'yes, I suppose I am.'

Pat nodded. She smiled slightly. I don't know whether she believed in what I do or not; after all, there are plenty who don't. But Pat was a nurse and along with poor rates of pay and a strong stomach, nurses have one thing in common: an open mind. You know why? Because nurses have seen everything. They have seen things that defy belief, that just don't make sense. They've witnessed tragedy and miracle in equal measure. Nurses don't scoff or sneer. They know far, far better than to do that.

'Well,' she said, 'I'm afraid you're probably right. She was given her Brompton's in the early hours, not long after her family brought her in. Her name is Anne. Shall we take a look?'

It wasn't castor oil that was dispensed on this ward any more. It was Brompton's Mixture. This is what they used to have in the old days, for the terminally ill. It was a morphine-based medicine that was administered to a dying patient on a spoon, a very, very strong dose of morphine, a fatal amount – the idea being to gently ease the dying cancer patient into death. They called it Brompton's Mixture because it was made at the Royal Brompton Hospital, where it was invented in the 1920s for use on patients with tuberculosis. I don't think it's used much nowadays.

With a swish, Pat drew back the curtain and we stepped inside. She turned to pull the curtain closed – *swish, swish* – screening us off from the rest of the ward. I got my first look at Anne. She lay, silent and still, on the bed, the sheet barely rising and falling as she breathed her very last breaths. Pat moved to one side of the bed, I moved to the other, so that we were on either side of her.

At the end of her bed sat a man. He looked at me and I at him.

Pat didn't see him, of course; he was in spirit. He was Anne's husband, I knew.

I was about to learn something very, very important about the ways of death and of the spirit world.

Two

The legacy of Waldemar...

Call me psychic, but I think I know why you're reading this book. Or one of the reasons at least. Because unless you've accidentally picked me up thinking I'm the latest Harry Potter (and if you did then you might want to think about a trip to the optician), you'll know a little bit about me. I'm a medium. If you want to call me a psychic, go ahead and be my guest; medium, psychic, it's all the same to me. But what it boils down to is this: I talk to the dead. And because of that I get asked one question more than any other. By clients, by those who come to my shows, by people who stop me in the street because they recognize me off the telly and, yes, by people who read my books.

What they want to know is, *What happens next?* They want to know, *Is there really such a thing as the afterlife?*

Well, get me started on the spirit world and it's difficult to stop me. My husband, John, would tell you that. I've had a lifetime dealing with spirits and the spirit world, so I know what I'm talking about. You know the film *The Sixth Sense?* I'm telling you, it's the story of my life. I'm like the little boy, Cole, in that: I see dead people. I talk to them.

But it's not so strange. I don't even think it's that unusual. It's my belief that we all have a bit of psychic in us. I'll go into this in a bit more detail later, but for now let's leave it at that: we all have psychic ability, it's just a case of having that ability teased out of us – of it somehow being discovered.

In my case, so much of what I am today is as a result of spending my childhood at a house in Fulham, on Waldemar Avenue, where I first discovered my gift. Oh God, the things I could tell you about life in that house. Not only was it full of spirits – as in, ghosts – it also, somehow, seemed inhabited by the spirit of my nanny. This was Nanny Gladys. She died when I was a very, very little girl, but she cast a long shadow – a shadow that remained with me throughout my childhood and in many ways still does. Though I don't remember much about her, what I do know is that she was beautiful. She was very tall and slim, with dark hair and eyes to match.

They called Nanny Gladys 'the witch of Fulham' because she had a way about her, and no, she didn't wear a pointy hat and carry a broom (although she did have two black cats who followed her about, called Topsy and Turvy – her familiars). She just 'knew' things, Nanny Gladys did.

She'd be standing at her newspaper pitch – she used to sell papers to city gents at the entrance to Putney Bridge Station – and there would be many times when, handing a newspaper to one of her customers, she'd pass on a hint, just a word or two that meant nothing to her but had enormous significance for the bowler-hatted gent purchasing his copy of the *Evening Standard*.

No word of a lie! Nanny Gladys playing the stock

market ... The difference was, she'd be doing it without even knowing she was doing it, which was something I came to recognize later in my own life, when the words would seem to fly from my mouth before I'd had a chance to clamp them tight behind my teeth. Words that meant nothing to me. Gibberish, really. 'That leaky tap's not doing your headaches any good.' But to the person standing there, some lady my mum had met in the street, for example, or a work colleague, they'd have great significance.

Well, that's something I got from Nanny Gladys. Her 'knowings'. Nanny Gladys would know if you were gay. If you were pregnant, Nanny Gladys could tell you whether you were having a boy or a girl. Not by feeling the bump or referring to old wives' tales: a low bump means it's a boy, or that kind of thing. She just *knew*. Just as she blurted out tips to the city gents – not even realizing what the words meant most of the time – she would blurt out this information to strangers. If you were gay and wanted to keep it a secret; if you were pregnant and you didn't want to know the sex of your baby ... Well, then it was best to steer clear of Nanny Gladys.

I wonder if Waldemar Avenue had as much effect on her – she lived there until her death – as it did on me.

It must have done. Oh my goodness, where on earth do you start? Well, I hated going upstairs. There was something in the bathroom, a naughty spirit that made me do things I have never told anyone about. I was too weak then. I hadn't learnt about my gift and about spirit world so I was open to manipulation from evil spirits and, I have to admit, I was well and truly manipulated by that spirit in the bathroom. It was by far the most malignant of all the ghosts roaming the house.

The lights used to go on and go off by themselves. At times it was as though I was controlling them. One day I heard a voice that shouted, 'Shut that bloody racket up,' even though there was nobody else in the house. (The racket was a Cliff Richard record. Sorry, Cliff, seems as though you're not a favourite in spirit world – at least, not with this particular spirit anyway.)

Next, I saw my great-grandmother Nanny Brodie in the outside toilet. This was the 1950s, remember. She told me to, 'Pull your knickers up.'

Funny. In spirit world, just as on earth plane, your loved ones never stop looking out for you.

I saw Mrs Spooner, too. Only, Mrs Spooner wasn't giving me advice to stop me getting a chill. Oh no – Mrs Spooner was dead on the stairs, her arms and legs all sticking out at wrong, grotesque angles, her eyes wide and staring.

When I told my mother what I'd seen, she gasped and put a hand to her throat. Turned out Mrs Spooner had died when Mum was pregnant with me – heavily pregnant. Mum had heard a scream from the hallway and come dashing out, only to see Mrs Spooner on the stairs. There was no way I could have known how Mrs Spooner had died – how she had looked and how her arms and legs were arranged; I was in the womb, for God's sake. Yet I had described the scene to my mum with absolute accuracy.

Well, it freaked Mum out, of course. Me? I'd seen the spirit of a dead lady on the stairs. You know what I did?

I went back to playing with my younger sister, Gina. The sight of poor, dead Mrs Spooner didn't bother me at all, for reasons I can't really explain. Why on earth wouldn't a little girl be terrified by a ghost? Especially one so horrific-looking as Mrs Spooner had been. But no. Then, as now, I accepted death. I suppose you could say I felt at ease with death, in the unpleasant and even gory aspects of it.

I saw spirits elsewhere, too. In fact, probably the very first spirit I ever saw was at nursery when I was just four years old. Looking back, I think this was the age at which I began to really become aware of my gift – of the fact that I could see and hear things that other people could not.

Reading all this, you might think I was a black-eyed, intense, scary child – like something out of a horror film, staring darkly at people from under my fringe and torturing dollies. Well, nothing could be further from the truth. Yes, times were hard: Fulham in the 1950s wasn't like it is now, all 4×4s and double mocha frappuccinos; no way could I afford to live there these days. We were hard up, and my mum and dad weren't exactly the most devoted parents in the world. Even so, I was mainly a happy-go-lucky, joyful child. What I mean is, I knew deep down that I was somehow 'different', but it's not like I sat there thinking much about myself. People didn't do that back then. You weren't constantly trying to 'find yourself'. There wasn't a quiz in a magazine: 'If you answered mainly Bs then you're probably a bit psychic.' You just got on with life; you didn't think of yourself as anything, really, certainly nothing 'special', like a medium or a psychic – I wouldn't be surprised if it never even occurred to Nanny Gladys that she might have been a psychic. That just wasn't the Fulham way. Well, not in our family anyway.

The other thing was, not only did I not talk about what I saw, I soon learnt not to even try. Most people either thought you were lying or a weirdo, so why bother? Might as well keep your mouth shut. Made for an easier life.

The only person who really listened was my mother. In the end, she took me to a spiritualist meeting at Kelvedon Hall, about fifteen minutes' walk from where we lived, and there – well, I don't want to sound boastful, but it was as though I was operating on a different, higher level to the other spiritualists. I was seeing things they couldn't see. I was able to tell them things about themselves I could not have known, having never met them before. That night I found something out about myself. I began to get an idea of what I could do. I began to realize that there were other people like me, but even they didn't see what I saw.

I never went back, though. I was fifteen at the time. I was more interested in the Beatles and boys and going to the pictures. Who wanted to hang around in stuffy church halls talking to dead relatives? Not me.

Then came work, kids, marriage, houses and mortgages and responsibilities and all the joy and heartache that comes hand in hand with living – all the stuff of a normal life, really, only mine came with frequent episodes of 'knowings' and spirit sightings.

By now, I was married to John, the love of my life – he

drives me up the wall most of the time, but I'd be lost without him – and I shocked him by seeing his childhood dog, Blackie. I think that was when he knew. I mean, when he really *believed* that I had this ability.

Even so, it never occurred to me that I could somehow make a living out of it. For a start, I couldn't really control it. What used to happen was this: I would be talking to someone and I'd see an image. So, for example, if I knew that somebody was about to come into money I might see notes floating around them. Other times, I would see that they had a person standing close to their shoulder. This, I now understand, is the spirit that always goes with them – we all have at least one.

Back then, I didn't realize that. I just saw ... *things*; I would suddenly know stuff I hadn't known before. It was just something that happened to me that freaked people out. It made them laugh, and it made me laugh because it would always take me by surprise. Most of the time, I was just as freaked out – if not more so – by some of the things I used to come out with. Sometimes it would make me howl with laughter. I'd have my hand to my mouth, thinking, *Oh my God, what on earth is all this?*

That was until I found I had the ability to control it. It all happened one day on New Malden High Street, and it was one of those situations where I was talking to a friend and she was telling me about the financial hardship she and her hubby were going through. Next thing you know, I had this image of her husband and money. And I switched it off. Just like a radio or a telly. One second the image was playing in front of my eyes, the next I switched it off. Like I'd been handed a Sally remote control.

That was it for me, really. Now, I call it opening and closing. If I'm working, on stage, doing the telly or doing a reading, then I can make a conscious decision to open, and I invite spirit world to give me messages. And they do, bless them.

If I'm not working – if I'm with my family, having a meal, sitting watching a film, shopping in Tesco, whatever – then I'm shut. The sign is up: Sally Morgan closed for business. And spirit world leaves me alone. They're very good like that, in the main. Very polite.

I still didn't consider trying to make any money from it, though. That would come in time, much later, after a business that John and I owned went to the wall and we were left literally penniless.

Then, and quite by accident really – which is the story of my life – I began doing readings from home and building up a client base. Word spread and eventually I found myself reading for the Princess of Wales and too many other celebrities to mention, touring the country with my show, meeting people and helping them to answer that one, burning question. The question they all want to know the answer to: *Is there an afterlife?*

Yes, love, yes there is.

Grab yourself a cup of tea, and I'll tell you all about it – starting with what I saw that day, back in 1979.

Three

Two spirits joined . . .

The spirit was dressed in dark clothing. He wore dark trousers and a jumper beneath a black jacket in the old style. Though he sat on the bed, he made no impression on the linen. His hands were placed either side of him so that the fingertips of his left hand were just inches away from the fingertips of Anne's left hand. Almost touching.

Looking back now, I think he was aware of me there. It's not like he was thinking, 'Hey up, there's a medium standing in here,' just that he knew.

I went over to Anne to speak to her.

One of the things we learnt during our training was how the body shuts down during death. We were told the hearing is the last of your senses to go. As nurses, we often used to speak to the recently deceased for that reason, so that the last voice in life they'd hear would be a soothing, friendly one.

I leant in close to her, passing a hand over her cheek. 'Your husband's come for you, Anne,' I said, ever so gently. 'He's here for you.'

I took hold of her hand. Her eyes fluttered slightly, just a tiny movement. Was that the ghost of a smile? And she died.

I looked up from the bed.

'She's gone,' I said to Pat, whose eyes widened slightly. 'She's gone with her husband, she left with her husband,' I said.

Pat reached for the crucifix she wore around her neck and kissed it. 'I think you're right.'

And this wasn't a psychic 'knowing' Pat was talking about. This was something that occurs quite frequently in the medical profession – especially among those who witness a lot of death. They can feel the spirit go. You ask a nurse. He or she will tell you. You get a sense of something leaving the body. Not so much at, say, road-side incidents, where there are all kinds of horrific trauma and it's very sudden. More on the ward, this is. Doctors and nurses get a feeling of the spirit leaving.

Me, I was discovering that I could do more than *feel* the spirit leave the body. Oh my God, I could *see* it.

Just as clearly as though I was watching TV, I saw the spirit leave her body.

How to describe it? Well, I don't know if you've ever seen the film *Ghost* – and if you haven't then I'll try not to give anything away – but my theory is that whoever wrote that spent a bit of time with a psychic. Because that scene when Patrick Swayze is lying in the street dying, and his spirit is out of his body, looking towards the light? Well, that light is exactly what appears. On my life. When I saw that scene I almost jumped out of my seat because there on film was the closest approximation of what I had seen on the ward that day.

Next, I saw the spirit. It seemed to rise from the chest. Not in human form as in *Ghost* – I guess they had to embellish it a lot for the film, it needs to work visually –

but as an energy, an essence, rising out of the chest and moving towards the light.

It was one of the most incredible, beautiful things I have ever seen, a new life beginning at the point of death. Or, perhaps, a new chapter of life beginning. I knew that I was being shown something so, so important about spirit world. And I felt enormously, incredibly privileged to witness it. I was seeing the soul leaving the body. I was observing the birth of a spirit.

I knew that spirit world existed, of course – I always had – but this felt like insider information. I was being shown, not that it existed – because I already believed in it anyway – but *how* it worked.

There was something else, too.

As Anne's spirit lifted from her body I felt a gentle, but very definite wind. No, not a wind – a breeze. Like sitting out in the garden on a summer's day, closing your eyes and turning your face towards the heat, feeling yourself cooled by a delicate breath of wind. It was like that.

And what I saw next was Anne joining her husband.

Though he had been in recognizable human form when I first walked through the curtain, now he assumed a different shape. Imagine a genie from a bottle, only in reverse: he was sitting there, then he became a breeze. Now they were both this vapour, almost like a luminescent gas, shimmering and really quite beautiful, and they came together, moved towards the light and left in the air above the bed. And they were gone.

He had waited to collect her, you see. That was what he was doing there when I first walked in: waiting to accept Anne into spirit world, to welcome her there, to guide her.

I realized then – and I truly, truly believe this, I'm as certain of it as I am of my own name – that nobody ever dies alone. There is always somebody there waiting to collect your soul. Some of us might have two or three, depending who we have loved in our lifetime and who has loved us. In Anne's case, she was a woman in her early seventies and she had been married and widowed, and I think it must have been a good marriage, because he was there to collect her. They were two souls made for each other.

It somehow feels wrong to admit I felt a kind of joy at seeing what I was seeing; after all, Anne's passing would bereave her family, cause them great sorrow. But I'd be lying to say different. To me, this was a revelation, a glorious confirmation of things I'd believed since childhood. I felt as though I was learning something, not just about spirit world, but also about the power of love. These two souls drawn together.

Here's something else I believe: those who come to collect us are those we have known and loved on earth plane – somebody you will feel safe with – because as a new spirit you need that comfort. You need the familiar.

So, say if John were to go before me (he won't, the bugger, I'll go before him, of course), then it would be John who I would see when I passed over. I'd be saying, 'Oh, hello, John, I am so glad you've come to meet me.' I would feel safe, comforted and reassured that it was John, the person I had loved most in life, who had come to welcome me to my death.

The reason for that is because souls have a magnetic sense to them. There is something inside you – and we'll call it the soul for want of a better word – that has a magnetic quality to it. And no, I'm not saying that iron filings will stick to you if you press them to your chest, but there is something there, something that has a gravitational pull. Touch your fist to your chest. In the middle. What do you feel? Do you feel the heat of your hand? Can you feel the knuckle of your thumb?

Where your knuckle is pressing, that is the home of the soul. It pulsates, it has a rhythm to it. When we die, our heart stops beating, our brain stops working. Both the brain and the heart are full of electrical activity. When they stop, they die, and the body dies with them. The soul, though, is different. It uses a different sort of energy altogether, it just doesn't work in the same way as the heart and the brain. It doesn't require the physical body as a host. So when the body dies, the soul has to leave the body – and that's what I saw. It has the same energy, the same essence as it did when the person was alive, and what it exhibits then is a gravitational pull to other souls – other people loved on earth plane, maybe even more than one at a time. If John died before me, for example, his energy would be shared between me and the children, in much the same way as a magnet will attract more than one object at once.

I watched Anne and her husband, joined in spirit, leave. Pat moved around the bed, performing what we called the obs – the observation – which is what nurses do when somebody has died. You check their vital statistics. She took her stethoscope, listened to Anne's heart, took her pulse. As she did so, she spoke to Anne, very, very gently.

'All right, my darling,' she whispered, 'everything is going to be OK. Everything is going to be all right, you're with the angels now. You're with the angels. I'm just going to lift your arm up . . .'

We both began the process of preparing the body. In those days, we had something called a deceased pack, and we would open it at the point of death. It was white, sterilized, and inside was a shroud, a name tag for the toe, cotton wool to pack the throat and genital areas, sterilized gloves, a plastic bowl to fill with water and cotton-wool pads for wiping the face of the body . . . How funny – I remember it all, just like it was yesterday.

And all the time we were doing this we were talking to her, comforting her. She sighed slightly as we busied ourselves around her, but we paid it no mind, it's not unusual for a body to do that when you move it. That's why people often think a nurse or a doctor has made a mistake, because air will escape from the body and the body will appear to make a noise. So when you wash the face of the recently deceased and you're pressing on their cheeks, air will often escape from their mouth and they can make a sound, like 'Oh.' They can even lift sometimes because of the air in the body.

Though I did the same as Pat, helping to comfort Anne, I knew something my colleague did not. I knew that Anne was no longer in need of comfort because her soul had joined that of her husband. She was in a different place now. A better one.

Four

A room at the Ritz . . .

For me, that afternoon represented a crucial step along the path of my learning about spirit world.

I had discovered something very important about the soul and how it leaves the body and I've had it confirmed to me countless times in the years, decades since, and that is: the process of dying is irrelevant. A person can throw themselves in front of a train or die aged 101, like the Queen Mother, in a beautiful, soft bed with servants all around, and it doesn't matter. However you die it is not to be feared because ultimately it means the same thing, it represents the same process: that of the spirit leaving the human form and moving on to the afterlife.

I see a lot of people who come to me with a terminal illness. What they want to know is: *Is it going to be OK? Is there life on the other side?* It's because they're forced to confront the reality of death – their own death – that they begin to question the process.

A lady came with her sister, who was terminally ill, to one of my shows in Bristol. She filled in a card that went into our 'psychic orb', which is a special bowl I use on stage into which go questions and requests from members of the audience. (Don't tell anyone, but it's actually a fish bowl from PetSmart.) Kevin, my manager, spoke to her. It turned out that her sister had a brain tumour.

During the show, I picked her card from the orb and gave her a reading. I don't recall much about the reading itself, save to say it was very emotional. What I do remember was that I met her afterwards. I end each show by sitting down, signing books. I'm pleased to say that I always have a large queue of people waiting to meet me (well, so far, fingers crossed!). After this particular show, I got to meet the lady and her terminally ill sister in person.

As we met, we shook hands and the sister said to me, 'Thank you so much, Sally. I only have a matter of weeks to live but you have given me so much hope. The readings and messages I witnessed tonight have made me certain that there is an afterlife.'

I nodded. 'Yes, darling, there is. Your soul will live and your soul will be with us. But listen, darling, it ain't over till the fat lady sings, and I'm not a singer.'

She laughed. 'Let's hope so,' she said. 'I can promise you one thing, though. I'll be here to see you next year. If not in person, then in spirit. I'll be on stage with you in spirit.'

She brought me to tears. Even John was tremendously moved, bless him.

Another time, I had a woman who came to talk to me and I immediately sensed a problem with her left side.

'I feel an impact,' I told her. 'Do you have something wrong with you, darling? Something seriously wrong?'

'Yes,' said the lady, 'yes, I do.'

As the reading went on it turned out she had terminal cancer. Clients never tell you these things up front – or, very rarely, at least. Even those who truly believe in what I do tend to keep their cards close to their chest, as though testing me. I understand that, I even approve. If you're in Tesco to pick up a box of eggs, you take a peek inside to make sure none of them are broken and they're not going to leak to all over your Weetabix on the way home. You check first – you check that something works because you're paying for it. And it's the same with me. Maybe you'd think that a lady with terminal cancer would want to discard all that, but not at all. This particular woman had a question to ask me. A question to which the answer meant more to her than anything. So of course she wanted to know if I was the real deal.

She had two sons and what she wanted to know was if she was going to be able to see her sons in the afterlife. She had just a few months to live.

'I'm only afraid of dying if I can't look down and see my sons,' she told me.

'You will, darling, you will.'

I remember it was one of those readings – you get them every now and again – when I needed time to myself afterwards. To have a little cry, a little think, pick up the phone and have a chat with my daughters.

It's always at once inspiring and very humbling to meet somebody who is facing imminent death. I consider myself very lucky and very privileged to be able to bring them solace and comfort during these last days. Over the years I have seen hundreds, if not thousands, of terminally ill people and their main question always concerns the afterlife. These are often people who have lived their lives without a faith. I see it a lot in men; they come to me feeling guilty.

I remember one middle-aged man saying to me, 'It's terrible, Sally, I have never believed up till now. I have always thought of mediums and psychics as being crackpots . . .'

'But now you want to believe, darling?'

'Yes. Yes, Sally, I want to believe because I won't be here in six months.'

'So, if I tell you that there is an afterlife, that you are going to another place after this one, will you be happy?'

He shifted uncomfortably. 'Well, no, not really. I need . . .'

'You need proof?'

'Yes.'

And this, I suppose, is where I really come into my own. I have the advantage, not only of being able to tell my clients that there is an afterlife – but of being able to prove it.

This man, Robert, had spirits with him: two women dressed in white, who were concerned for him. They were his aunts and he took messages from them. He wanted to know, 'Will it be painful?'

'No,' I told him, 'you do not feel a thing when you die, not a thing. Dying is like that.'

Although we abandon our physical form when we cross over, spirits often take on physical form in order to communicate with me. It happens an awful lot – I would say about ninety per cent of the time – that they take on some kind of recognizable human shape in order to pass messages to me.

'I can see your mum,' I'll say. 'She's got red glasses on and she has long, black hair. And, oh my God, you and she were so alike.'

Spirit world is so good like that. They will try – not always successfully, I might add – to make things easy for me. At the least, to try to help themselves be identified. I really think they do this so that the person I'm reading for will know for certain that I have the right spirit.

My belief is that everybody has a date on their forehead. Not a literal mark on their face, but a metaphorical date of death. On that day you are going to die. By hook or by crook, even if you stay in bed all day, something's either going to come through your ceiling and land straight on your head, you're going to choke on a bit of your lunch or you're going to trip on your way to the loo. Your destiny on that day is to die. Sorry, but that *is* the day you're going to die.

So what you find is a great acceptance of death in the afterlife, if that makes sense. Spirits certainly don't dwell on the manner of their death and if I'm talking to a spirit who's been murdered and they tell me, 'I have had my throat cut,' the chances are they'll say it either for the purposes of validation or because it has some bearing on the message they want to pass across. But how they died has no effect on their actual *character* in spirit world.

People are often amazed by this. Not long ago, I was on stage and this exact thing happened. I had a spirit come through who had been the victim of a violent, fatal assault.

Do you know what he said to me?

'I'm very happy.'

Now, I know that his family members in the audience took a great deal of comfort from that comment. On the other hand, I also know that other audience members found it a little difficult to swallow. How can somebody who was so brutally murdered possibly be happy in the afterlife? Surely they should be consumed with hatred and torn apart by a desire for revenge?

Not a bit of it. His soul had gone to a better place. To heaven, if you like. I'll talk about that soon – about spirit world, what it is and what happens there. But for the time being, suffice to say it is a place of love. It is a better place than earth plane. So there's no reason for the soul to be unhappy. It's a bit like being turfed out of your B&B and being given a room at the Ritz.

When I talk to spirits I very often get a feeling of intense warmth or euphoria. It will start from my feet and go all the way up my body – this incredible, warm sensation, a feeling of completeness, of security.

That feeling is a tiny fraction of what they are experiencing on the other side.

The idea of an afterlife is certainly very comforting, whether you have a terminal disease or not. Don't get me wrong, though, I would still be totally bereft, completely, utterly insane with grief, if anything happened to those I love. Even with all this knowledge. I would still mourn and cry and grieve. Why? Because I'm a human being. Even though I have no doubt that there is an afterlife and even with all my first-hand experience, I would still be out of my head with sadness. Because if the doctor told me tomorrow that I only had two years to live I am not sure that the idea of an afterlife would be much consolation. I wouldn't fear it, at least, but that doesn't mean I'd be happy to relocate there. After all, I still have so much to do on earth plane. I want to move house, I want some donkeys. I want this, I want that. Only two bleeding years to do it in? No thank you.

I think the point I'm trying to make is that we are on earth plane for a reason, all of us, and while we're here, we need to make the most of our time. We owe it to ourselves to enjoy all that it has to offer us. We need to love and be loved and not be frightened of passing over. We should live our lives knowing that earth is simply the first stop on the journey of the soul. And there is a long, long way to go yet.

People often ask me what I will do when I reach spirit world. It makes me laugh, that question, because I don't really know the answer. I tell you one thing, though, there isn't a day goes by when I don't think, *Oh my God, when I get to spirit world what are they all going to say?* Because the thing is, I haven't been able to please everyone. I imagine spirits approaching me with 'Hey, you, you know when you were talking to that girl in Croydon, why didn't you say such-and-such?' I could be in hot water, I can tell you. I imagine having to explain myself to the spirits: 'I'm sorry! There is only one of me you know.'

They won't mind. There's total forgiveness in the afterlife. This is why you rarely find spirits who are bitter about the manner in which they've died, even if they've been the victim of violence, for example. After all, any violence inflicted upon us on earth plane is done to our bodies and in spirit world the physical form has no relevance. We don't take it with us. We don't have a likeness. As spirits we cease to care about such things. In these circumstances it is not only easy to forgive what has been done to us on earth plane – it's pretty much vital.

Five

'She sleeps with my killer . . .'

It happened in Blackburn. I was on stage giving readings.

Now, what happens when I am on stage is that I have many, many spirits crowding around me, both on stage and moving among the audience, all wanting to pass messages to those on earth plane.

It can be really difficult during a show as there are so many spirits, all clamouring for attention. There is so much information hanging in the air. It can be like trying to listen to ten different radios all playing different stations at the same time. I have to tune nine of them out in order to concentrate on giving somebody in the audience a decent reading. At times it can be very, very tough indeed. It's why, if you see me on tour, you'll see me move quite rapidly from one half of the auditorium to the other. All the time, I'm trying to filter the voices. I am trying to concentrate on one message. I am trying to listen to the most distinct voices.

Inevitably, this means that some spirits are ignored. Most are very polite. Some are not so. Some will be very forward. Some will hang back. What usually happens is that the further we get through the show, the more voices come through. I have my own theories about this, and one of them is that I warm up. Like a footballer or, perhaps more accurately, an old TV, I don't work so well on a cold start. I need to be warm and open and spirit world needs to know that.

One particular spirit was most persistent. As I continued with the show, he remained just behind my shoulder. Imagine you're having a meal and there's a waiter hovering behind you. You can't see him, but you sense him; you're aware that he wants something.

This spirit was like that. As I began to pick things up about him, I started to realize why. He had an important message. It came to me that he had been murdered.

'There is a woman in the audience who is the girlfriend of my killer,' he told me. 'He's told her what he's done. He's told her that he murdered somebody. That somebody was me.'

The message stayed in my head – either that or he repeated it – because it nagged at me for about half an hour. As we came to the end of the first half, my little inner voice was telling me, 'You've got to say it, Sal. You've got to give the message.'

It was as though the words were trying to burst out of my mouth. On the one hand I was desperate to give the poor man's message. On the other hand ... what if I was wrong? What if I was misinterpreting the message?

After all, it happens all of the time: voices are indistinct, the things spirits say jumbled and confused.

Also, voices and messages can get mixed up. Remember what I was saying about the radio? Can you imagine trying to listen to twenty news broadcasters at the same time? You're bound to mishear things, and I do.

Obviously, if I'm giving a reading in my office there are fewer spirits vying for attention, but even then things are never truly cut and dried. On stage? Well, you can imagine . . .

Oh God, Sal, I thought. *What if you've got this wrong? You're going to look a right fool. You're possibly going to upset somebody. You might make a terrible mistake.*

All of this was going through my head as I continued with the show until, seconds before the lights went down for the interval, I could hold back no longer.

'Ladies and gentlemen,' I said, 'just before I go, I've got to tell you something. I have a man on stage who has been the victim of a murder.'

There was an audible gasp from the audience. I could see people looking at one another. I found myself scanning the faces, trying to pick out the right person. If I was right, this girl was in there somewhere.

As I spoke, the spirit came more sharply into focus, as though floating from the back of the stage into my eyeline.

'She knows my murderer,' he said. 'She sleeps with my killer. He will do it again. You must tell her he will do it again.'

For the first time I saw him and knew what had happened.

He wore dark clothing and stood holding his ear. One side of his head was completely caved in. At the same time as I saw him, I knew what had happened to him. Without being told, I just 'knew' . . .

I knew that no one had ever been caught for the murder. I knew that someone was sitting in the audience who knew the man's murderer. I knew he'd had his head kicked in. That he had been beaten to death.

I could sense that it had happened in the street. I had the impression of darkness. I could feel that it was a senseless attack. As though the men involved just felt like getting hold of somebody and the victim had simply been in the wrong place at the wrong time. Oh, the poor man, dying like that, alone and frightened, torn from his loved ones in such a brutal manner.

'The man I have on stage was beaten to death,' I said.

In the audience, hands went to mouths. Another gasp.

'Look,' I continued, 'you might find this a bit difficult to get your head around but, believe you me, nobody is as shocked as I am. He's telling me that the girlfriend of his killer is in the audience tonight.'

There was another sharp intake of breath.

You could have heard a pin drop.

'He has told me that she knows. The girlfriend of the killer knows.' I looked at the audience. I let my gaze travel across the stalls, then up to the circle.

'She's in here somewhere,' I said, pausing a moment, then, 'I'm talking to you now, darling. I know you haven't done anything wrong, but I need to ask you this: can you live with yourself? Can you live with yourself, because the spirit I have here is telling me that your boyfriend will do it again.'

I let that information settle as hundreds of faces looked back at me. 'My crew are at the back of the house if you wish to go to them and I will see you personally. I promise you that. I will speak to you personally.'

That's not something I normally do. But I felt a need to do my best by this poor man.

The interval was twenty minutes. I went to my dressing room, where I sat composing myself. Shortly after I'd arrived came a knock at the door and it was one of the crew with an audience member. She came into the dressing room and we got chatting. However, it soon became clear she wasn't who my spirit wanted to contact. She turned out to have a friend-of-a-friend who said she knew somebody who had been murdered.

'Thanks for coming, love, that was very, very brave of you,' I said as she left.

Minutes later, I had another visitor, another girl, this one shaking, very nervous.

But speaking to her, once again, it wasn't my girl. This was about a friend of her mother's. Her son had been murdered and she knew the murderer but the police wouldn't do anything. My heart ached for them, but there was nothing I could do. Once again I thanked her for coming. Once again I marvelled at how brave she had been to come forward.

But not the right girl.

I glanced at the clock. Just five minutes of the interval left.

Perhaps I was wrong? Perhaps I had got the message wrong? Maybe the spirit had made a mistake?

Then, with literally minutes to go before the second half, came a knock at my door . . .

John is one of those who stays front of house while I'm on tour. He sells programmes or takes cards for the psychic orb. He doesn't usually come into the auditorium during the performance. As I sat in my dressing room during the interval he was in the merchandise kiosk with another member of the crew, Oliver, neither of them aware of what had happened just before the break, when a girl approached them.

'Are you a member of the crew?' she said.

Oliver said, 'Yes, can I help you?'

She said, 'No, I don't want to speak to you. I want to speak to him,' and she pointed at John.

Then she started talking about a murder.

Well, John thought she was a bit of a crackpot at first; he didn't know what she was talking about. Instead, he directed her towards my manager, Kevin.

Somewhere between John and Kevin, she had a change of heart and decided she didn't want to talk to me. She spoke to Kevin, but only to say that she'd changed her mind.

Kevin came to see me.

'Sal,' he said, 'we had one other woman come to us in the interval but she's changed her mind. Sorry. Can you use one of the others?'

Kevin, bless him. It's his job to get me on and off stage, to make sure each night is special for the audience. We have over a thousand people in there, and we have to make it a great show for everybody, not just one of them. But I couldn't talk to one of the others. Not if it wasn't the right girl. I owed it to the man on stage with me.

Then all of a sudden it came to me.

'*It was her*,' I said, making myself jump with the force of my reaction. Somehow the spirit was still feeding me information.

'It's her,' I told Kevin. 'It's the girl who changed her mind. I know it's her.'

'Sorry, Sal, she doesn't want to talk. I'm really not sure there's a lot we can do about that . . .'

I placed my hands on the dressing table, thinking, *It was her.*

I couldn't let go. I needed that validation. Like in an American soap opera, I needed 'closure'.

'I can't believe it,' I said to Kevin. 'It was her, I'm sure of it.'

I had to speak to this girl. I knew I had to speak to her. One thing I found myself certain of was that this girl was planning on seeing the murderer again and it bothered me. It really bothered me as I went on for the second half, which I normally begin with a little talk about my life story, just to warm up my voice, to adjust to the audience again.

But not on this occasion. I went on, the house lights down, and I said, 'Now, I left you in the first half with a man on stage in spirit who was telling me that there's a woman in the audience who knows his murderer. Well, we've had some reaction to the murdered man that I have on stage here. In fact, we've had three young women come forward.'

The audience said a collective, 'Oh my God.'

When you think about it, it is pretty scary to think that in an audience of around a thousand, three of them believe they know a murderer. Goodness me, how many murderers are there?

I said, 'I'm not going to say a name, but I do feel you sitting in the audience. You've got to trust me, everyone.

33

Two of the people who came forward, they are very brave, and my heart goes out to them, and I want to thank them very much indeed, but it's not them. The third girl. It's you, darling. You are the one this spirit wants to address. He's a lovely young man, darling. He was. Once. He's not angry with you, darling, he just wants to talk. Now I know you don't want to be identified, but...'

There was a voice from the darkness.

'Sally. Sally, yes, I will.'

I swear, every single face in that entire theatre turned towards the woman. I got her to stand. We put a camera on her.

She was in her mid twenties. Certainly no older than thirty, with straight, blonde hair. Her clothes were plain. She wore a denim skirt, a T-shirt top.

Later, when I talked about her to John, he described her as looking very agitated, like she didn't know what to do with herself. It was interesting, actually, because when she first approached John and Oliver, though she had no idea that John was my husband, it was him she chose to speak to. Oliver is an ex-policeman, so perhaps she had a sixth sense, a feeling about that. I wondered then if she perhaps had a little ability herself. Perhaps the spirit saw the connection.

'Do I know you?' I asked her when the audience buzz had died down. 'Have I ever met you?'

'No,' she said.

'And you're the third lady who came forward?' I asked.

'Yes.'

'But you didn't want to talk to me before?'

'No,' she said. 'One minute I did, Sally, the next minute I didn't.'

'Well, darling, I'm glad you did,' I said, 'really glad.'

She nodded. Everybody in the entire theatre was hanging on every word. Blown up large on the screen, she looked nervous, agitated, eyes darting around.

'Do you mind telling the audience why it is you think you're the person I want?'

'My boyfriend told me that he murdered someone,' she said.

A gasp from the audience.

'It's your ex-boyfriend, isn't it?' I said to her.

'Yes,' she said.

'Do you know how he murdered this person?' I asked.

She didn't answer. For some reason, she stood motionless, just staring at me, her eyes getting larger and larger.

She knows, I thought. She knows.

'Because I know. The man I have standing here has told me that he was kicked in the head. What killed him was a kick to the head. Does that mean anything to you?'

It did. The words hit her as though she'd been slapped.

'Yes,' she said.

'Why?' I said.

'My ex-boyfriend is a kickboxer.'

I have never heard a sound like it in the theatre. The whole audience gasped as one.

Now I was getting more from the spirit.

'The spirit I have here is saying something about spark,' I said. 'He goes off like a spark. Is that it? Does that mean anything to you?'

Her hand flew to her face.

35

'Oh my God,' she said after a moment or so, taking her hand away, 'my ex-boyfriend's nickname is Sparkle.'

There was an incredible electricity in the venue. I think we all realized that something quite remarkable was happening.

The killer, he had just been showing off, I saw now. Because he was a kickboxer, he had been trying to impress his mates, jumping in the air, launching himself at the victim.

I pointed at her. I suppose you could say I became quite cross with her, saying to her, 'You don't know what you have on your shoulders. He's transferred his guilt on to you. You cannot get into bed with him again knowing what he's done to this man. Knowing what he did with two other men watching. He kicked that man's head in. That man – the man I have standing here – was somebody's son. He had a family who loved him and they do not have closure because his murderer, who you sleep with, has not been caught.'

I could definitely tell that, though he was her ex-boyfriend, he had been in touch with her again. My impression was that he wanted to get back with her.

'He told you in bed, didn't he? One night?'

'Yes,' she said. 'How do you know that?'

I said, 'Because I know. Because the victim is telling me.'

I said to her, 'How do you feel about the victim coming to see you?'

You could tell she didn't know what to say. People in the audience were nodding. The whole time, the spirit on stage, the victim, was watching. I felt his presence there and I felt a kind of gratitude coming off him. As I spoke to the girl it was almost as if I became him, I was his mouthpiece.

'Do you know what I am being told?' I said to her. 'The spirit is telling me that your ex is going to do it again. He's going to kill again. He has enough anger in him to do this again because he's got away with it.'

She was nodding, close to tears, and I decided that she'd had enough. It wasn't her who had killed this young man. In many ways she was simply another victim in the whole sorry affair. I thanked her for her bravery, she sat down and I continued with the show.

She didn't hang around afterwards, unfortunately. My crew were scurrying about trying to get hold of her, but she scarpered, pretty sharpish.

It is my belief that she will eventually go to the police to tell them what she knows. It's not likely to happen soon, unfortunately. But one day it will.

I think that the spirit was able to help, in a way. At the very least I hope that what he said will have stopped her from going back to her ex-boyfriend. But also, perhaps, what she experienced that night will have relieved the burden – at least some of it – of guilt she had on her shoulders. It was obvious to look at her that she carried it. John saw it, in her nervy manner. Kevin detected it. I certainly did. And anybody who saw her face on the screen that night will have seen the face of someone who was haunted, not by a spirit, but by a living presence: her ex-boyfriend and by what he had done – and what he was capable of.

And isn't that ironic? We think of being haunted

and we immediately think of being bothered by a ghost. Yet the spirit who stood at my side on stage that night came not for purposes of revenge, or even something so humble as the pursuit of justice. No, actually what he wanted to do was help this girl, relieve her of some of the guilt crushing her. And, hopefully, somehow stop the attacker striking again.

It can be really difficult to get your head around the fact that at no point was the victim motivated by either revenge or any sense of earth-plane justice. And I think this is where a lot of other mediums, as well as lay people, go wrong. What they do is apply the values that we have on earth plane to spirit world.

It's an easy mistake to make. Moreover, it is an attractive, appealing idea. After all, we've seen it in films and on TV: the idea of the spirit driven by revenge, even after death. But it doesn't work that way. When we place earth-plane values into spirit world we are trying to mould something to make it fit. You can't. It's like clipping back a tree to try to make it look like your *idea* of a tree.

You can't do that. Even if, when fully grown, the tree is ugly and ungainly, then you just have to accept it. There is a reason the tree has grown that way. You cannot expect to understand the reason – it just is.

It's the same on the other side.

What I'm saying is, his motive for appearing that night was pure and simple love.

I cannot give spirit world any higher accolade than that really. Love is the fuel upon which it runs. Which is perhaps why I am able to cope with what can be quite traumatic readings such as that one and another one, which I often say was the most challenging of my career to date ...

To tell you about that one, I'll need to talk about my TV show and how I became *Star Psychic*.

Six

Happier with a cup of tea and a biscuit...

It all seems like such a long time ago now. Like most things, it began with a phone call. This one was from Anna Richardson, who worked as a producer for Celador at the time. She had wanted to make a programme about a psychic. Apparently, whenever the subject came up my name was mentioned, so in the end she gave me a call: 'Can I come and see you?'

I had just returned from America where I had been making a film (the less said about that the better), so I showed her some rushes of it, and she was impressed with those. Plus I told her something about her personal life that no one could possibly have known, that blew her away (and no, I'm not going to say what it was, because Anna's a very well-known TV presenter these days. You've probably seen her on Channel Four, doing *Supersize vs Superskinny* and *The Sex Education Show*. So I'll spare her blushes) and more or less there on the spot she asked if I would do a programme for Celador.

Yes, I said, I'd definitely be interested – depending on the programme.

Then, next thing you know, Anna had left Celador. That's the way it is in TV, I suppose, but I didn't really mind, things were going well for me: I had my practice, a huge client base, a healthy waiting list. It would have been nice to be on the telly, of course, but it's not like I was ever desperate to be famous. Still not. Happier with a cup of tea and a biscuit, I am.

So I forgot about it.

Anna didn't. She ended up at another company where she started to develop the programme. Its working title? *Medium at Large*. She explained the proposed format. Was I still interested?

I thought about it for two seconds. Actually, maybe it was only one-and-a-half seconds. Yes, I said.

Because for the last fifteen years I'd been asked to do at least three projects a year for TV, and they were all virtually the same. I'd always turned down anything that involved being in a haunted house waiting for a ghost, for example. I think you know the kind of thing I mean. Another time, I was asked to do a programme where I would give readings for objects. In the tests I got good results but because they wanted to film my hand vibrating and shaking over the object I wouldn't do it. That's not how I work. I don't go into a trance, or shake, or even close my eyes. I just don't do any of those circus tricks. And fake them for the camera? No thanks.

With Anna, things were different. I knew immediately that she 'got' me. I wanted us to come up with an idea that stretched me, that showed the viewers a little bit more about my ability than just standing there in front of an audience seeing spirits. She wanted the same. She wanted to put me on TV and she wanted me to be *me*. There was a big problem though, and it was something I'd run into doing the odd bit of TV over the years, appearing on topical programmes, when I would usually be accompanied by a sceptic, sitting on the sofa beside me.

This was all to do with ITC rulings, which limit what you can do with mediums on television. Basically, the rulings state that demonstrations of psychic practices are only acceptable as part of factual programming and then as part of a legitimate investigation.

Luckily, the ITC ruling is aimed at programmes about the occult, because what they don't want to see is the occult being used for entertainment purposes.

Now, you know me, I'm not exactly your average devil worshipper, am I? I'm a grandmother. I get my shopping at Tesco. I bicker with my husband over whose turn it is to make the tea. I'm just not your occult type. Or, if I am, then I suppose I'm the *acceptable* face of the occult. I think if I had been a 25-year-old girl, really career-minded, very attractive, who also had this incredible ability, then maybe they would have taken a different view. It would have looked witchy and sinister, perhaps. But with me, I was the same on telly as I am in the flesh, just like, 'Oh, come here, darling, let me give you a hug.' Everyone says to me when they meet me, 'Oh, I wish you were my mum.' I bring that out in people, and that's what the production company responded to, it was what they wanted. Plus, Anna's other half, Charles, came up with a so-simple-it's-genius idea. He said if we had a voiceover throughout the programme saying 'Sally "believes" she can speak to dead people', or 'Sally "believes" she can read from this item', then we could get round the ruling that way.

So, they went into pre-production. I wasn't involved

with that bit of the process, having made it very clear right from the beginning that I wanted to know nothing about who I was going to see or what was going to happen. That way nobody could say, 'She was primed.' Because I wasn't – the whole thing was done under the strictest possible conditions, so my only input was taking the odd phone call. Anna would say, 'How do you feel about us putting you in a house? Up the road will be a telephone box and we'll have a hotline to the telephone box. Could you read for the person in the telephone box without seeing them?'

I'd say, 'Well, I'll give it a go.'

And that was one of the challenges we ended up using. It was a pedestrianized road in the West End, and I sat in a room in an office and at the other end of the street, around a corner, was a public telephone booth, which I couldn't see, maybe half a mile away. It was to show that I could do readings over the telephone – which I do, in my work, all of the time.

One day Anna said to me, 'How about if we got some famous people and we gave them a reading?'

'Sure,' I said, the way I responded to almost all of her ideas, 'I'll give it a go.'

It ended up working a treat, of course. Plus it gave us a new title: the name of the programme went from *Medium at Large* to *Star Psychic*, a name none of us liked at first, but it grew on us.

After that, it was a case of making a pilot programme, which is what you do to convince the heads of channels to commission a whole series. And that's when the madness really began.

Seven

First-night nerves . . .

The night before the first day of filming I lay in bed.

Oh my God, Sal, I thought, *you've bitten off more than you can chew here.*

You know what? I have never told anyone that, not even John.

Why, though? Why was I nervous? The television company – 21st Century Fox – were being lovely. They were ringing me, telling me how excited they were. Plus, I was looking forward to getting out of the house. I was thinking, *Great, I'm going to be meeting people.* I love meeting people, I absolutely love it. So every single day would be an adventure. Neither was I worried about any challenges they might throw my way. In my naivety I had said to them, whatever you want to do, I'll give it a go – even though I had no idea what each day had in store.

When you're making a TV show – and I think it's the same with film – everybody involved on that day's shoot, from the runner to the director, gets a call sheet. Not me. Because of the secrecy, all I would get was an email telling me what the day was, what time the runner was picking me up, what time I was having lunch and what time I would be coming home. That was it. I wouldn't even know whether I was going to be in the studio or outside.

The only thing I really knew was whether I would be in London or outside it. I wasn't even allowed into the production office, because they had storyboards in there. On the rare occasion I went to HQ I was relegated to sitting in the reception area.

So, I was lying there thinking, *Will I look like a silly old lady? A fruitbat trying to prove herself?*

The thing is, I've never wanted to appear *desperate* with my ability. I have never felt any great need to prove it to the doubters. But would I look like that now?

Plus, would it work? Yes, on the one hand I was looking forward to getting out and about – getting out of my office for once. But, on the other hand, my office was my sanctuary. I suppose there is a little bit of superstition that goes with what I do, and I certainly feel that readings tend to work if I'm in the office. It's ridiculous – I know it is – because when the office is being decorated I've been happy enough doing readings in the kitchen or in the front room. Even so, my mind was clouded with what they had in store for me. I didn't know what to expect, remember. All I had to go on were those few phone calls with Anna. I had an idea, I suppose, but not quite enough to calm my nerves.

'Make sure you bring two or three changes of clothing, will you?' Anna had said to me. I didn't realize why at the time, but of course I was soon to find out. One of the first things I learnt about the filming process is that they piece it all together. We would do a day of telephone readings, then a day of Internet readings and then a day in the studio. These segments would all be cut up and distributed throughout the series so that it looked as if

I went from one challenge to another like some kind of psychic superhero in my Sallymobile.

Sorry to spoil the illusion. I mean, when you think about it, it makes absolute sense to do it in chunks, for all kinds of practical and financial reasons. It just seems a bit – I don't know – a bit *boring* to do it that way, I suppose, and it certainly made for some long and arduous days of filming. Plus, of course, I had to change clothing between every challenge.

The next day, a car arrived. It was my runner. Runners don't actually run everywhere, that's just what they're called. Mine was named Nat, and she drove a people carrier. Over the coming months I'd be seeing an awful lot of Nat; I'd be spending an awful lot of time being driven around by her. Nat, if you're reading, you are a truly lovely girl, darling, but forgive me if I tell you that you make a better runner than you do a driver. My God, the amount of times young Nat almost killed us both. Once, she drove all the way from my house to Shaftesbury Avenue with the handbrake on and the hire car nearly went up in flames. I could see the smoke, she got out and lifted the bonnet and there were flames everywhere.

Tell you what, though, the poor girl was worked off her feet. I live on the outskirts of London. It takes a good two hours to get into town in the rush hour, so in order to get me on set on time Nat would have to arrive at all hours of the morning. Seven a.m.? That was a lie-in for me. Most days, Nat would turn up about 5 a.m. And that was *at my house* at 5 a.m. God only knows what time she had to get up and get out of her own place. I guess

I should forgive her the odd near miss in the circumstances.

While Nat's job was to make sure that I was fed and
watered and ferried from place to place, she was also the
runner for the entire production. So if somebody wanted
coffee or some lunch, she would fetch it. That's how
they all start in TV. Who knows? She'll probably be
reading the news in five years' time. Anyway, she was my
Girl Friday.

That first day, she took us to Spitalfields, where I met
the crew. There were twenty-two people involved in the
production of *Star Psychic*, and I think most of them were
there on that first day, buzzing around, preparing to
begin filming. We had two or three cameras, hand-held
ones, and there was a bit of setting-up in the street but
not too much, as they wanted to keep things looking very
real. They wanted this edgy, on-the-fly feel to the whole
show, so whenever we filmed in the street they made a
real effort not to impact on their surroundings too much.
What you don't really want is too many people hanging
around; you want members of the public in the background looking as natural as possible, not gawping at you.
It was always a bit of a balancing act.

Anyway, when we got there I went to a café in Spitalfields which was really nice, one of those organic places
where you get different sorts of lovely bread and you can
have bacon rolls. By this time, it was about 8 a.m. The
first familiar face to arrive was Anna.

'Hi, Sally!' *Mwah mwah*. Lots of air kissing going on,
of course. She was wearing a green parka with a fur
collar and what I was soon to discover about television

production crews – especially television production crews filming at a cold Spitalfields market at eight o'clock in the morning – is that they all wear green parkas with fur collars. They're standard issue. Plus, they all carry clipboards. If you ever want to infiltrate a television production crew, wear a green parka, carry a clipboard and a cup of coffee, and you'll fit right in.

'Oh, this is really exciting,' said Anna. 'Now, you're going to meet the director.' She lowered her voice, whispered in my ear – 'The director is Charles, my other half. I live with him.'

Right, I thought, assuming that because I got on so well with Anna, and because Anna was clearly a great admirer of my work and believed in what I do, that her partner would be the same.

Oh my gawd, was I wrong about that.

He was a complete non-believer. Utter cynic. Total sceptic. Oh great.

Let me tell you something about sceptics. They're hard work. They have a different belief to me, which is fine, absolutely fine. They obviously think I'm faking it. Well, that's a bit annoying, but I expect if somebody claims to be doing something you don't believe in, then you must think that they're faking it. So I suppose I just have to accept that. And they can be dreadfully self-righteous too, and slightly joyless and almost always terribly sarcastic.

Charles was no different.

He, too, was wearing a green parka with a fur collar. He was holding a can of Coca-Cola and smoking. What I was to discover about him was that he had to have a can of Coca-Cola and a fag on the go all of the time. That was his diet. God only knows what his insides must have been like. I dread to think.

Also I had the suspicion that he didn't like me. He obviously didn't believe in what I do and it didn't seem as though he was prepared to give me the benefit of the doubt as a person either.

Charles wanted to chuck me in at the deep end. So, having met the crew, we got straight down to business.

'What do you want me to do?' I asked him. I hoped I didn't look as jittery as I felt.

He looked at me, mouth curling somewhat. 'We want you to do readings. Isn't that what you do?'

Goodness, he was a sarcastic one. 'Yes,' I said, smiling, 'that's what I do, Charlie.'

This is a great start, I thought. *I've already fallen out with my director . . .*

Eight

Silly old bat . . .

They sat me down outside the café and set up cameras on the other side of the road. The idea of having the cameras across the street was to get the scene looking very naturalistic, a bit like a documentary, with passers-by walking across the camera. They had two cameras. One trained on me, the other on the person I would be reading for. That way, they could get both of us at the same time then edit us together later, so they get my reading, followed by the reaction of the person I'm reading for. It's called coverage.

Anna spoke to me. She said, 'OK, we have a girl who would like a reading from you, her name is Karen.' A girl took a seat in the chair opposite me. Young, smiling. I picked up something about her immediately.

'Right,' I said to Anna, trying to sound oh-so professional, 'just a normal reading?'

'Yes.'

'Just as I would in my office?'

'Yes.'

'No holds barred?'

'No.'

'Are you sure?'

'Yes, of course. Why?'

'Well, because she's going to cry.'

Anna looked at me, surprised. 'She's going to cry?'

'Yes.'

'How do you know?'

'Anna, I'm a psychic, remember?'

'Ah,' she said, clicking her fingers, 'right, yes.'

Anna scurried back over the road to speak to Charles, to tell him what I'd said. I saw him confer with the cameramen and they made some adjustments. I now know that what they did was train the camera on Karen's face.

Who still sat opposite me, of course. What she thought of all this I have no idea. No doubt, she was thinking, 'Silly old bat, what does she mean I'm going to cry? Of course I'm not going to cry . . .'

I looked at her and she returned my gaze, biting her lip. I wondered if she was as nervous as I was. 'Look, darling,' I said, 'don't worry, it's only a camera. Ignore it. Just look at me. It'll be all right.'

She was a pretty little thing. She wore a dark coat and one of those hats with flaps that come down at the side like rabbit ears. She was hunched over the table slightly, rubbing her hands together to warm them up. Goodness only knows what we were doing sitting outside a café on such a cold morning. Must have been mad.

'Do you know when this is going to go out?' she asked.

Yet another of the things I would discover about working on a TV show – everybody always wants to know when it's going to go out; nobody on the show has a clue. Understandably, members of the public want a date and a start time and possibly even some idea of exactly when they will appear. Equally understandably, everybody on the TV show just wants to get the bloody thing made in time. And, anyway, it's not up to them.

Me, I was more worried about Karen. And I'm quite proud to be able to say this, but throughout the making of the programme – as with all of my readings – I was always concerned about the people involved. I always put them above the making of the show.

From across the road, Charles called, 'Action.'

(And you'd have to have a hard heart not to feel a thrill hearing that word said in the flesh – to hear it said about you.)

I looked across the table at Karen. On the other side of the road the cameras were going. This was it.

'Why am I picking up that you're concerned about where you're going to be living?' I said to her. 'There's America. I'm picking up something about your dad in America. What's that?'

She burst into tears.

It turned out that her mum and dad were divorced. Her dad lived in America and she lived with her mum, but recently her mum had fallen in love with another man and gone to live with him, leaving Karen by herself. She was only nineteen, the poor little thing, now living on her own. Her dad didn't want to know. She'd phoned her dad that morning and he hadn't been interested. 'You can't come over and live with me and my new family,' he'd told her.

And I picked up all of it. She was absolutely devastated and, as the reading ended, she was in my arms, sobbing, me doing my best to console her.

After we'd finished, I gave her a cuddle just before she left. Karen was as pleased as punch with her reading, I knew that. Even though she was crying she was grateful to have somebody to talk to, which I guess is the function of the medium. Because I'm guided by spirit world I can go in straight to the root of the problem. It's like talking to a confidant, I suppose, like having an instant impartial best friend. Someone who understands your problem, who can share it with you. Even so, as I watched her go, I turned to Anna as she approached the table.

'Oh God,' I said, 'I feel dreadful. That poor girl. We've just taken her off the street and I've made her cry.'

I was acutely aware, you see, that there was no follow-up. Usually when I deal with clients the service is much like that of counsellor. I will be seeing them the following week, or the following month, so we're able to work on things together.

Meanwhile, of course, the crew were absolutely over the moon. I mean, it sounds really mercenary, but they want tears. It's so visual. So . . .

'It was absolutely brilliant, Sal,' said Anna. 'Absolutely superb.'

During the next reading, the girl was in tears again. In fact, practically every reading I had that morning was a good one. Hit after hit after hit.

That was how I gained the respect of Charles. Looking back now, I think he was finding his feet in the same way I was. I came on set looking at him like he was God, because he was the director. But what I quickly realized was that we were just two people who do what we do – we both have equal talent in our own arena. Once he'd seen me in action, and seen that I could deliver the goods, and I had learnt to call him Charles (memo to self: Charles hates being called Charlie), we began to get on.

I'm not sure whether he then became a believer in what I do. Probably not. But he knew I could do 'something', and whatever that something was worked on telly.

Filming continued. The next day, we worked more smoothly together and after three or four days we were operating as quite an effective little team. I think I proved to be fairly flexible for them – anything they threw my way, I'd give it a try – and in the end there was only one challenge that I refused to do.

This was a task where I would read for two men and every time I got something right, they would take off an item of clothing. The idea was that by the end of the task these two hunky, good-looking guys would be naked in front of me.

Sounds like great fun, eh? Well, on the one hand, yes. But, to be honest, I just wasn't comfortable about it. These were guys in their twenties. I mean, I've got son-in-laws that age, so it just didn't seem appropriate. I hated it, to be honest, so I called a halt to it.

Unfortunately, we'd got as far as actually doing the challenge. Like all the street challenges, everything was genuine. Every person I read for during the show was real. None of them were actors or set up. For the studio-based challenges, the crew canvassed volunteers by posting messages on websites: 'Do you fancy appearing in a psychic show? Have you lost anyone? Would you like to appear in a revolutionary new psychic show?' That kind of thing.

But these guys had been pulled off the street on the day. They were taking off their clothes. It was done in Borough Market in London and there were passers-by shouting out lewd comments. There was some kind of festival going on into the bargain and everyone was drunk, including the two guys – well, you're not going to take off your clothes on television if you haven't had a bit of Dutch courage, are you? But that went against my personal code, too, because I never read for people who are inebriated in any way.

Still, that was the only hiccup.

It took a week to make the pilot, at which point they took it to ITV, where we met a controller called Matthew Littleford.

I'll never, ever forget it. We met him in a café next to ITV centre.

'We want ten one-hour shows,' he said.

Anna's eyes widened. 'Pardon?' she said.

'We want them now,' he added.

I could see Anna trying to process this information. And we're talking about Anna Richardson here. She's a woman who really, really knows her TV. Incredibly clever, driven and very, very canny. It takes a lot to phase her, but here she was – well and truly phased.

'What do you mean, you want them now?' she managed at last.

He must have been loving this. 'We want to start making them now. You've got to go into pre-production straight away.'

John had been waiting in the car. Like all men, he's a

real slave to his bladder, and he'd been sitting out there dying for a wee, bless him. Unable to hold it in a second longer, he'd wandered into the café hoping to use the loo. He met us as we were hurrying down the stairs.

'Oh, hello,' he said. 'Everything all right?'

I introduced him to Matthew and gave him the good news. 'Oh, Sal, that's wonderful, love,' he said, 'Well done, love,' and for a moment or two we looked at each other on the stairs. We've been through a lot together, me and John. More than most, I dare say. It meant a lot, that moment.

Beside me Anna had gone a funny colour. She didn't even say a word to John, just 'I've got to go, I've got to start work.'

And she dashed off, the phone already clamped to her ear. A couple of weeks later we began filming the series.

Nine

'He's out of his head on cocaine and he stinks of kebabs . . .'

In all, it took four months of filming to complete two series of the show. The turnaround was so quick that we were still filming when it was first broadcast. To get it done, we were working fifteen hours a day, every day, and let me tell you, it was hard work. You've heard stars telling you that it's not glamorous making a film or TV show, haven't you? Then imagine how unglamorous it is making a TV show in record time on a very limited budget.

For a start, I'm very particular. I mean, I'm not vain but I always like to look nice, and having a shower at 1 a.m. before you go to bed to get rid of all the grime, then having another one at 4 a.m. before you go out again – let's just say that's not me. If that's your idea of glamour, fine. It ain't mine. What's more, I like my sleep. I'm not really a morning person. So 4 a.m. mornings? Freezing cold and bone-tired, I used to stare at myself in the mirror and croak, 'Nothing is worth this. Nothing.'

Plus, you're always eating on the go, and you have to eat with the crew. You can't be precious about your food. Now, John would tell you how much I love my food. I think of myself as a real foodie, so eating in McDonald's day in day out just isn't for me. There were times when I'd have to say to the crew, 'Guys, I'd love to eat with you, but I really can't stomach another burger. I've had it up to here with fast food.'

These guys would look at me like I was mad.

'Look, I just want a salad, OK?'

And I'd toddle off to Marks & Sparks to get myself a yummy salad, leaving the crew trudging off to Burger King or wherever.

But you can't do that all the time. It would seem rude. So, I had my fair share of Burger King and McDonald's.

And, of course, the trouble with having a runner who does the running for the whole production was that she was needed all the time. Which meant I had to arrive on set when she did. So even if I wasn't needed for four hours of setting-up time, I still had to be there, and that meant a lot of waiting around. I remember one night, it was about 7 p.m., freezing cold, and I was sitting outside a house for hours on end while they tried to sort out a problem with the lighting. Turns out it was the Cheeky Girls' house.

And at the end of the day I would have to wait long after they'd finished filming to go home, sometimes until all the rigging was taken down. Then Nat would take me back, drop me off at midnight.

Now, poor old Nat; she then had to go to Chiswick, deliver the tapes, drop off some cameras sometimes, then go back to where she lived, which I think was Marble Arch, then she'd be at my house the following morning for 6 a.m. again. Poor old Nat, I can't say it enough. She started off this beautiful young thing; four months later, she was a wreck. I mean, it was hard for everyone; with a production like that, you have to give blood – or, rather, they *expect* you to give blood – and there was a lot of illness, a lot of people simply couldn't take the pace of it. But of everybody on that crew, poor little Nat suffered the most.

Matters weren't helped by some of the celebrity readings that didn't quite go according to plan.

To be honest, the biggest problem there was that the celebrities had never heard of me, so assumed I was a fortune teller. They came along expecting end-of-the-pier stuff: 'cross my palm with silver'. Stuff they could have a laugh about. Inevitably, within minutes of the reading beginning, they would suddenly realize that I wasn't some kind of crank.

As a result, there were several celebrities who refused to allow their readings to be broadcast. Or whose readings couldn't be shown, simply because there was too much sensitive information coming out. One of those was a singer called Pearl Lowe, who was married to a member of the band Supergrass and was well known as a member of the infamous 'Primrose Hill set'. Don't worry if you haven't heard of her – I hadn't either.

I'd begun the reading when I saw a great darkness around her. 'Oh my God, darling,' I said, 'you've had something dreadful happen to you. You were molested . . .'

All of a sudden, a publicist, who up until that moment had been sitting quietly in a corner of the room, jabbing away at her BlackBerry, jumped up like we'd just attached electrodes to her body.

'Stop!' she screeched. '*Stop!*'

'What on earth is the bloody matter?' growled Charles, coming out from behind the camera.

'How have you read the manuscript?' demanded the publicist. She stared accusingly at me, then at Charles, then back at me.

'What is she talking about?' said Charles to me.

'What are you talking about?' I said to the publicist.

I literally had no idea.

'We've got a book coming out,' panicked the publicist.

Still it was as clear as mud. It seemed to take hours to establish that I hadn't read any manuscript; that, in fact, until about half an hour ago, I had no idea who Pearl Lowe even was.

In the end, Pearl took me to one side. She'd been blown away. 'This is great stuff,' she said, 'I want this to go on.'

Behind her, I swear, the publicist was having kittens, but we eventually got it together enough to sit down and continue with the reading. She confirmed that she had been sexually assaulted.

After that, there was another issue – completely separate – regarding the paternity of her daughter, Daisy. It turned out that Daisy's father was Gavin Rossdale, the singer with a band called Bush, who was going out with another singer called Gwen Stefani (No? Me neither). The reason I can tell you all this is because it ended up being splashed all over the papers. A member of our crew – we have no idea who it was and still don't – went to the *News of the World* with the story.

The upshot of all this was that the *News of the World* had

themselves a great story and they did a deal with Pearl Lowe's people for exclusivity, which meant that we couldn't show it. Great shame.

One of the most memorable readings – for all the wrong reasons – was an ex-member of a very famous boy band. The crew had hired a casino in the centre of London and had done the place up like a James Bond set. I had been asked to wear a long black dress, as though for a night out, and there were extras wandering around. The celebrity – let's call him Dave – was supposed to be dressed up like James Bond, too. The idea was to look high-class, urbane, sophisticated.

It didn't quite go to plan.

As I arrived on set, Anna came running up to me. Remember, at this point I didn't know who the celebrity was (and, if I'm honest, even when I found out I still didn't know who he was). Anyway, Anna comes running up.

'Oh my God,' she gasped, 'the celebrity you're reading for, it's a fella, and he's been out all night, he's been in a fight, he's out of his head on cocaine and he stinks of kebabs. What on earth are we going to do?'

I looked across the casino and saw him slouched behind the roulette table. Oh my, what a state. Not even 8 a.m. yet and this guy was in a terrible condition. He had a big black eye, his nose had been flattened and he had a cut on his lip, which was still dripping blood – all over the collar of his white shirt. A sorry, sorry sight. He didn't look much like James Bond, I can tell you.

'Oh, darling,' I said, approaching where he sat, 'have

you been hit by a car? What on earth has happened to you?'

(I still didn't recognize him, but then, he was covered in blood and bruises . . .)

He just looked at me. There was nothing behind the eyes, no reaction at all. Make-up people were circling him, wielding powder and looking apprehensive, but he was batting them away as though he couldn't stand anybody to be near him. He just sat there, dripping with blood, whiffing of takeaway, sniffing slightly.

'I don't think we can film this,' said Charles, coming over, throwing a contemptuous look at Dave.

Me, him and Anna went into a huddle. 'Look,' said Anna, 'let's just do it. We've hired all this crew, we have all these extras walking around, we have to do something here.'

Then – and I could hardly believe it – I felt something. I started picking things up.

'Start the cameras,' I said, walking over to the table and sitting down opposite him. Dave indicated the roulette wheel in front of him.

'What number shall I put it on?' he said.

'Twenty-six,' I said, quick as a flash, without even knowing why or how the number had appeared in my head. They span the wheel and the number twenty-six came up. Trouble was, the crew hadn't got the cameras running, so the moment was lost, which didn't do much to improve the general mood.

Still, we thought, we'd struggle on. We were just about to continue and start the reading afresh, and Charles had shouted 'Action', when Dave insisted on stopping proceedings.

'I need a coffee,' he croaked.

'Come on, Dave,' sighed Charles from behind the camera. 'We're rolling. Let's get some footage then we can stop for a break.'

'No,' stated Dave, 'we're stopping now. I need a coffee.' His eyes, bloodshot and red-rimmed, had shrunk to tiny black dots in his face.

'Where is that bloody manager?' I heard Charles mutter under his breath. They had been trying to get hold of Dave's manager all morning with no success. Little wonder – the manager probably knew exactly what was happening and wanted to steer well clear.

So, we stopped while somebody (Nat, probably) fetched Dave's coffee.

Dave sipped his coffee gingerly, hands shaking slightly as he did so. His face was now a slightly grey colour, I noticed. Under the lights he'd begun to sweat and his forehead had acquired a thick, oily sheen. Some pin-up.

Then we attempted to resume the reading. I was still open, still picking things up about Dave, Charles had shouted 'Action', and then . . .

'I need to go to the bathroom,' said Dave flatly.

Charles shouted 'Cut'.

'Come on, Dave,' Charles said, still, remarkably, keeping his cool. How he managed that, I'll never know. 'Couldn't it wait? Can you tie a knot in it, mate?'

There was a pause as everybody hung on Dave's next words. We all knew that if he went to the loo, that was that. The way he was sniffing, it was obvious it wasn't a wee he needed.

'Sorry, mate,' replied Dave, 'when a man's got to go, a man's got to go.'

Charles spread his hands in defeat. The crew let out a collective sigh. I think we knew then that all was lost. Sure enough, when he came back from the loo – having spent about twenty minutes in there – he was in an even worse state than before: slurring his words, unsteady, with sweat pouring off him. There was no point in continuing.

Charles abandoned all attempts at diplomacy.

'Get him out of my sight,' he shouted. 'I can't bear to look at him any more.'

And that was that. The ex-member of the boy band left the casino, never to be seen again.

Others: the model Nell McAndrew was a little too guarded and cautious and didn't make for a great reading. The weather girl Andrea McLean had a change of heart after her reading had become a little too personal. Jeremy Edwards was canned for similar reasons.

All of these problems paled into insignificance, though, compared to the life-changing reading that was to follow. Not only was it the most distressing reading of the show, it was probably the most distressing of my entire career.

Ten

The belly dancer . . .

It happened towards the beginning of the filming. I had my email as usual, this one telling me I was going to a studio in Wimbledon just up the road from where I live. *Lovely*, I thought. *A bit of a lie-in.*

I should have been feeling great. So why in the morning did I wake up petrified?

I shook John's shoulder and he grunted.

'John, John, wake up,' I said.

He grunted some more.

'I don't want to go to do the show,' I told him. 'For some reason – I can't work out why – I just don't want to go today.'

'Well don't go then, love,' he said.

'Don't be *stupid*, I've got to go,' I said, sighing.

'But you've just said . . .' he mumbled.

Yes, yes, I know what I just said, I thought, dragging myself out of bed. Why is it that men just don't understand?

So it was that, an hour or so later, Nat turned up as usual.

You shouldn't really ignore a feeling of foreboding. That's the spirits trying to tell you something. I'd like to say I never do. I mean, you'd think, as a medium, I would be much, much better at translating these messages from spirit world and I guess I am, for the most part. But I'm as prone to moods and dark thoughts as anybody else. And it's not always possible to say whether a feeling like that is a genuine message or a chemical imbalance. Just because I'm more open to them doesn't mean I always act upon them. To digress for a second, not that long ago I was on my way to Gravesend to do a show and I saw an owl. It was during this snowy weather we had at the beginning of 2009 and we were on the motorway. I was looking at fields rushing past and I saw a fox cross a field and then, in a tree, I saw an owl.

I said straight away to John, 'Oh my God, we're going to hear about somebody dying. I saw an owl. An owl in the daytime means death.'

I just knew. The sight of the owl – I just knew. That weekend we heard that a friend of ours, Sara Roache, the wife of the *Coronation Street* actor Bill Roache, had died.

This Saturday morning before filming though, was different. I just had this feeling that something wasn't right. I think if I'm honest, I actually thought that it might be something to do with Nat's driving – sorry, love – but we arrived at the studio in Wimbledon safely and still the feeling hadn't gone.

It was a little studio that was hired out for the day, and I was ushered straight into the dressing room. I was never allowed on the set on these occasions – not until the very second that I was needed – in case I got a glimpse of the challenge being set up. Usually, with about ten minutes to go before I was needed, somebody would arrive at the door and say, 'Sal, you're on in ten minutes.'

I always used to say, 'OK, can you tell me what's happening yet?'

'Sorry, no, we'll tell you when you get there.'

And that's exactly what happened on this occasion. I walked from my dressing room into the studio, which was in what they call 'white-out', which means the floor was white and there were white screens around, too.

I remember there were a lot of people in the studio. There must have been at least thirty of them, more than our normal crew – they used to hire extra people in on certain occasions. Plus, there were cameras everywhere. They even had cameras on the ceiling. I found out later that we were doing a challenge that involved me matching dogs to their owners, and for this they wanted to film the dogs from above.

They had a screen in the studio. Standing nearby was a man dressed in black trousers with no top on. Just a white collar and bow tie. Alarm bells started to ring. I was already thinking of that business at Borough Market.

'Anna, this isn't anything sleazy, is it?'

Perhaps that was at the root of this strange feeling . . . ?

He was just there to stand beside me, as it turned out. A sort of butler-minder character, needed for one duty in particular.

'This young man here will blindfold you,' explained Anna. 'Behind that screen are people who will approach you one by one. You hold their hands and tell us what you pick up about them. What we want to do is see if you can pick up their job. When you've done that you can take off your blindfold and have a look at them. How does that sound?'

Well, it was at least a challenge I knew I could do. Don't ask me how, but it's something that spirit world helps me with. I don't actually see spirits; in a situation like that, it would be all about my knowings. I can touch the person, or look at a picture of them, or listen to them over the phone or on a tape, and pick up things about them. One of those things can be their career. Certainly, if a person has a very clearly defined job, like fireman, or policeman, then I would expect to be able to pick that up straight away. It depends on the job. If a person works with computers, say, I would expect to know that, but not necessarily whether they worked in 'project management' or 'systems implementation', if that makes sense. It's as though each person has an imprint of what they are and the clearer the imprint, the more I'm able to read it.

'Right,' said Anna, 'give us your glasses, Sal.' She indicated to the butler bloke. 'Get it on her.'

On went the blindfold. The world went black. Whatever it was they were using to blindfold me, it was doing the job all right. I couldn't see a thing. For a second or so I fought a wave of disorientation. Here I was, unable to see, standing in the middle of a studio, with crew buzzing around me. It was a strange and not altogether pleasant feeling. What made it worse, of course, was that my earlier sense of foreboding had returned. And it had returned with a wallop. I found myself shaking slightly. When I tried to swallow it was as though I had a piece of dry toast lodged in my throat. *Come on, Sal*, I thought, *pull yourself together*.

It would always take about ten minutes to get going, after my arrival on set. There would be lots of, 'Could you stand there, Sally?' and, 'Let's just try this light on you, Sally.' Everything has to be perfect before they start the cameras, so you just have to wait. The whole time, feeling the same sense of foreboding. My mind was chewing over the possibilities. Was it just something I'd eaten? Was it a challenge later in the day? Near me, I heard Johnny, the assistant producer, a lovely Irish man. 'Are you all right, Sal?' he asked.

'Not really, Johnny,' I said. 'I feel very uncomfortable about something – something is going to happen . . .'

'Oh, Sally, what are you picking up?'

'I don't know what I'm picking up,' I said, sounding sharper than I actually meant to. 'I don't know what I'm picking up, I just know there's something here that I'm not going to like.'

Later, they told me they thought it was the dogs. Obviously, they knew that my next challenge involved reading dogs and they put my nerves down to that. Looking back on it now, had I known that there were going to be dogs there I might have put it down to that, too, because I've never read for animals. As it turned out, of course, it wasn't the dogs.

What on earth was up with me? I had been filming now for about a fortnight, I was used to all this. I shouldn't be feeling this way. Why was I shaking?

'Anna?' I called. 'Anna? Are you there?'

I found I wanted a friendly voice nearby. I wanted to know that Anna was standing within reach. I was desperate to ward off this strange, isolated feeling I was getting.

'Just coming, Sal,' she called, sounding as though she were on the other side of the studio.

Keep calm, keep calm, I told myself. I heard her approaching.

'You all right, love?'

'This challenge,' I said, hoping my voice didn't betray my nerves, 'there's nothing unusual about it, is there?'

'No. Why?'

'You promise? You're not trying to pull a fast one, are you?' I tried to laugh, hoping to keep things light.

'No, don't worry, darling, all above board, you'll be great, don't worry,' she said, squeezing my arm slightly before withdrawing. I heard Charles barking out orders. I heard the *click-fizz* sound of him opening a can of Coca-Cola – always a sign that he was ready to start rolling.

'OK, everybody in position,' he said, 'then . . . action.'

My head filled with noise, with blackness. *This could be it*, I thought, *the source of the fear*. Perhaps it was happening . . .

I heard footsteps coming towards me. I was open, picking things up, my head crowded with sensory input. I suddenly had a tremendous desire to tear off the blindfold but resisted – just – holding it together – *just* – for the sake of the filming.

It must be because it's the first one, I told myself. *Yes, that must be it.* The footsteps stopped right in front of me. And suddenly it all made sense. Everything clicked into place. I knew exactly why I had woken up that morning with a sense of foreboding. I knew precisely why I had been so nervous, shaking, experiencing such dread. Everything had been leading up to this moment.

I felt hands hold mine and, with a jolt, I was torn out of my body and forced elsewhere.

I found myself seeing a room. Not just seeing it. I was *inside* it. It was dirty and grimy, cold and smelly. In a corner lay a naked woman, curled up on the floor in a foetal position. To the right of me stood four men, arranged almost exactly like the cameramen in the studio. The four men held cameras. They had been using them to film the woman. There was a fifth man in the room.

The fifth man was me.

I looked down and could see my hands, only they were not mine, not Sally Morgan's hands. They belonged to somebody else, the fifth man.

I was scared, trying to control it. I had never experienced anything like this before, becoming another person like this. I tried to command my body: *Give me my hands back. They do not belong to you, they belong to me.*

And also, amazingly, I was still mindful of the programme. Still thinking, *You've got to say something here, Sal. They're filming you.*

(They're filming you.)

They filmed her.

All of a sudden I knew exactly what had taken place in that room. The five men had raped the woman. They'd filmed it.

It all clicked. The room was a garage. On the other side of it was a car and I could smell oil. I think it was a lock-up, a place where people repaired cars. I had the impression that it was underneath something, perhaps underneath a railway in the arches like you get in Waterloo, only this definitely wasn't in the UK. I had the sense that it was an eastern European country. Bulgaria, somewhere like that. The filming had been taking place on cine cameras erected on tripods, as well as standard single-picture cameras, the click-click type.

I felt myself absorbed in the emotions in the room. I could feel the pain of the woman on the floor and suddenly I wanted to sob, just as she was. I wanted to weep because men had pinned me down and raped me.

At last I pulled myself together. 'Although I'm here to tell you what you do for a living,' I said, 'which most definitely has something to do with movement and dance and possibly singing, I have to tell you that I'm completely overwhelmed, because I'm feeling a lot of sorrow here.'

'Yes,' she said.

'Because I think a man – or some men – have done something really bad to you.'

'Yes,' she replied. Brave, brave thing.

'I'm so sorry. I feel you've been raped.'

'Yes,' I heard her say. 'Yes.'

'Oh my God, and we've got cameramen here today. They filmed you, didn't they?'

'Yes.'

I looked towards the camera – still with my blindfold on, still holding her hand – and said, 'He filmed you too, didn't he?'

Poor old Pete, the cameraman, blurted out, 'Not me.' Which might seem like an odd thing to say, but you have to imagine the sudden change in atmosphere that descended on the studio. You could have heard a pin drop. It was as though everybody in the room was holding their breath.

In the wake of Pete's outburst there was a moment

when it looked like filming would stop. Then Charles said, 'Keep rolling, keep rolling . . .'

She was eighteen when she was put through this ordeal. This had happened in another country and suddenly I got the sense that it could have been so, so much worse. I sensed that there were men in the room who wanted to kill her – like making a snuff movie – but that she was saved by other men in the room who wanted nothing to do with her death.

Oh, thank God.

Yes, at least three men in the room who wanted to kill her. I looked down at my hands and saw that they were folding up a sheet of tarpaulin. They had put her on rubber sheeting during the act. Why? Because they didn't want to do it on the stone floor. Not for her sake, for their own. Now they wanted all of the evidence to be destroyed, so they had hosed down the tarpaulin and hosed her down as well.

'I need to get this really tight,' I thought, 'because I have got to get this in the boot of my car.'

I realized with a lurch of horror that I had been thinking the thoughts of the rapist. I was either in his head or he was in my head. Did that mean he was dead? I don't know. All I know is that I had never before experienced such complete immersion. I have never seen my own body change like that. I had never found myself thinking another person's thoughts. And to have this happen with a rapist – a potential killer. It was all I could do not to vomit.

Finally, I couldn't take it any more. I ripped off the blindfold and at last clapped eyes on her.

From her clothes I could see that she was a belly dancer. She was a pretty thing, with wide, wise eyes that had seen too much sadness, known far too much pain. She smiled. I could sense that she had reconciled herself to her ordeal. There was something in her eyes and in her smile that told me so; the way she clasped my hand, gently rubbing as though to comfort me.

Even so, I couldn't handle it. I broke down, almost hysterical. They had to shut down filming for an hour and a half while I composed myself in my dressing room. After that – well, what's the saying? The show must go on. It had cost a fortune to hire the studio, the extra crew members needed and everything else. And we had to continue filming. I came back out to see the rest of the guys behind the screen. (They changed the order in which I saw them before the broadcast, so that the belly dancer was last, but that's not the way it actually happened.) I was still a bit dazed and in shock, really, and I didn't correctly get a diving instructor. The rest I got, though: a nurse, a fireman and a chef. The chef was an interesting case, actually.

Sceptics love to try to pick holes in what I do, and one of the ways they try to explain away that particular challenge was by claiming I was able to see either through or below my blindfold.

Well, that's the biggest laugh ever. For a start, I wasn't wearing my glasses, and I can't see a thing without my glasses. Even if I had been able to see through the blindfold, quite frankly it wouldn't have done me a lot of good. The guys behind the screen were dressed in their work clothes because it's TV, and TV is a visual medium. Nothing to do with giving me a helping hand, I can tell you. But here's the thing. Say that I was able to see through my blindfold. Let's just say. Then how did I know he had suffered from a knife injury in his shoulder? How did I know he was a pastry chef? How did I know he lived above a pub? Couldn't have seen any of that through the blindfold, could I?

It was nice, in a way, to get back into my comfort zone, because with the belly dancer – well, that vision took me so far out of it. I had found myself knowing all kinds of terrible details – objects the men had used, things they had said – which, even though it was in a foreign language, I somehow understood. It was incredibly harrowing.

Some of the other readings that I found very difficult to get through were the Internet readings, which were done over two or three-day period. They were all incredibly emotional and all were about loved ones who had died under very tragic circumstances. When I began each reading I had no idea whether I was going to get a murder, suicide, accident or whatever. By the second day, however, I had worked out that, whatever happened, it was going to be very emotionally draining.

They did them in what they call a location house, houses you can hire for the day. I had a bedroom that I used at the top of the house and the people who came in for the Internet readings were situated in a kitchen area; the TV people made sure we never met. I used to think, *Oh my God, how brave are these people?*

I think, in the end, it really took its toll on everybody making the programme.

The thing was, would all our hard work be rewarded?

Eleven

A standing ovation

I'll never forget the premiere. They hired a cinema in Leicester Square and everybody involved in making the programme was invited to watch it as it was shown for the very first time.

Can you believe that? We hadn't even finished making it – there were at least two days of filming left and I had to go right back to work the very next day – and here it was being broadcast.

I had no idea how it was going to look. I'd seen the odd bit of footage here and there, but not enough to form an opinion. Anna kept saying to me, 'You're going to be so surprised. I think you're going to love it, I really do.' That was all I had to go on.

I knew they had multiple editing suites hard at work on *Star Psychic* because it was such a quick turnaround. Usually they have just the one editing suite, but because we were making the programme so quickly they'd hired out six, all working 24/7 to turn it around. I got to meet the editors that night at the cinema in Leicester Square. They came rushing over to me. One of them, a very tall man, said to me, 'You don't know us, but we know you really well.'

I said, 'Oh my God, why is that then?'

He said, 'Because we see you every day.'

He was joined by a colleague, who said, 'When I come into work every day, I've got a smile on my face as soon as I walk in the building, because I can hear your laughter from the editing suites.'

Apparently, you couldn't move around the building without seeing me. God, the poor dears.

'Do you know what?' another said to me, moments later.

'No, what?' I said, still feeling a thousand feet tall.

'We have as much on the cutting-room floor that's as good as what's gone out. You're quite difficult to edit, to be honest, because it's all such great stuff.'

There were about 250 people in the cinema all told. Of course, I had no idea what the turnout was going to be like before I arrived. Had I known, I probably would have stayed at home. Too nervous, you see.

I took my seat among the audience. Charles and the other bigwigs sat on chairs in front of the screen, giving little speeches and talking about the making of the series. Sitting next to me was a man I didn't know, so I introduced myself.

'Oh, I know who you are,' he said.

'Oh, do you?'

The lights went down, the show about to start.

'Oh yes,' he said. 'I wrote the music for your show.'

'Has it got music?' I almost shrieked.

He was sitting next to his partner, and the two of them burst out laughing. 'Yes,' he said, 'of course it's got music.'

I nudged John, who was sitting on the other side of me, lowering my voice: 'John, John – it's got music.'

This is how totally clueless I was.

Then the programme was broadcast.

At first, the people in the cinema were laughing and cheering. The second guest was Danny Dyer, who was hilarious, everybody loved him, and there were girls there swooning over him: 'Ah, I love Danny Dyer,' they were saying and, I have to admit, I thought it would continue in that vein, be a bit jokey. I didn't really mind as everyone seemed to be enjoying themselves, but I was keeping my fingers crossed that it wouldn't turn out to be – oh, I don't know – *flippant*, I suppose. Not just for my sake, but for the sake of those who had agreed to take part, those brave souls who had agreed to Internet readings, the belly dancer and others.

They didn't let me down as it became more serious, especially for the first Internet reading. John told me later that he looked around and saw that people in the audience were crying.

When it was over, I was given a standing ovation. Everybody was shouting, 'Speech, speech,' and I stood up from my seat, feeling very proud and just a little embarrassed.

'Oh, thank you, everyone.' They cheered. 'I don't know what I'm meant to say really,' I added. Instead I smiled and waved and plopped back down into my seat as quickly as possible.

Next, we all trooped off to the aftershow party and there, people looked at me differently; everybody knew that we had captured something extraordinary.

And sure enough, the public thought so, too.

The show has to go out after the watershed because

of the subject matter, so the first series was broadcast on ITV2 after 9 p.m., but it won its share of the audience in that time slot. They repeated it at midnight on the same night. For one show I had nearly three-quarters of a million people watching it at half past eleven at night, which in this day and age, with so many channels and so much to choose from, is a massive share of the audience. Then it went to ITV1, again winning its audience share. It has been absolutely amazing. And when Harry Hill picked up on it, it gave us another boost. I'm regularly asked if I minded Harry Hill sending me up on his programme and the honest answer is: not a bit of it. He's such a funny man – he had me in stitches – plus he sent me a lovely card and, let's face it, you can't buy advertising like that, can you?

Since then, I just haven't stopped. The show has led to more TV appearances, more offers and, most importantly, my live show. It was completely life-changing. What stuck with me, though, was the power of some of the readings, and what stayed with me the most – and still does, actually – was the reading with the belly dancer.

Twelve

What I know about spirit world

It was the spirits who told me about the belly dancer. They told me about the girl in Blackburn, too. In fact, they're behind every message I get from the other side. Every message, every knowing, every precognition – I get it all from them and they give it to me for one reason.

Because they want to help. Because they want to give comfort, reassurance, hope and advice to those of us on earth plane.

I'll give you a for-instance. At one show I had a man in spirit who came to me a long time before I went on, and ended up being the first message I dealt with. I galloped through the introduction during which I let the audience know what to expect, before saying, 'Listen, I've got a lovely man who's been with me now for the last hour and he keeps saying to me, "Look up", and his name is Rob, or Bob, Robert. I think he wants a woman, he's saying Col, but it's not Colin.'

A lady made herself known and she was passed a microphone.

'Are you called Col?' I asked her.

'Colette,' she said.

'Now, the man I've got here, I don't think he's a relative, is that right?'

'No,' she said, 'he's a dear friend of the family who's passed.'

He was very keen to make contact, I could tell. Desperate to tell them how pleased he was they'd come that night. Next, he wanted me to let them know that he was at peace on the other side.

'He's in no more pain,' I told Colette. 'He's saying to me, "I was ready. There was no more that could be done. I closed my eyes and went to sleep," he says to me. Now, I can tell that the very end for this man was incredibly peaceful, but I think in the months leading up to his passing he would have been very uncomfortable. He's telling me that he didn't want any more treatments either, does that make sense?'

Colette was nodding in recognition.

Next he gave me another name. 'Who is Liz?' I said.

'My sister,' said Colette.

'He also mentions the name Carol,' I said. 'Who's that?'

'My other sister.'

He was a good family friend, it turned out, and he missed all three of them very much. What I loved about that message was the kind of ripple effect it would have created, because Colette would have gone home and told her sisters about the message, and just imagine how much comfort it would have brought to them. It makes me dizzy to think.

During another show, I was looking for a Di, or a Dido – an unusual name – who had a connection with a 'Lizzie' in spirit.

A hand went up and the microphone went to a lady in the audience who told us her name was Dids. She had lost someone close to her called Lizzie, who stood with me on stage, who told me there was a lot of pain involved in her passing. 'But I'm free of pain,' she said, 'it's gone, no more.'

I passed the message on to Dids, but even as Dids – a right character, lovely, she was – was reacting, Lizzie was telling me something else.

'Now she's talking about New Zealand,' I went on. 'Why is that, Dids? Lizzie wants you to go to New Zealand.'

'My kids live in New Zealand,' she replied. 'She was very fond of them.'

Lizzie urged me to tell her. 'You should go, darling,' I said. 'You should go to New Zealand.'

'I can't believe you're saying this, Sally,' she said, laughing, eyes shining. 'It's all so true.'

'Well, that's what we're here for, darling.'

Now, not only was Lizzie, in spirit, trying to give Dids advice, she also wanted to give her reassurance about her passing.

'She was so frightened of dying,' said Dids.

'Her feet were lovely and warm before she died,' I told her, 'and she died surrounded by God and by heaven and real proper angels. People who really loved her. They didn't want her to suffer any more.'

Dids smiled, and in fact it ended up being one of the best messages of the evening. They often are, those kind of readings, I think because they show spirit world at its very best: a place where the only currency is love; where they watch over us to bring comfort and closure to those of us on earth.

This is what they do in spirit world. You might say it's their job. And they do it until it is their turn to move on, at which point they undertake the next stage in their journey – towards a place in spirit world I think of as Divinity.

Now, before I go any further, one mistake I don't want to make is to give you the impression that I know it all. Because I don't.

I think as mediums there's a pressure on us to have a ready reply for everything, much more so than any other occupation. If we meet a question with the reply, 'I don't know', it's as if we're admitting we're making it all up. Rather than do that, there are many people in my line of work who feel they have to come up with an answer – one that 'fits'.

Not me. I don't interpret and I don't edit on behalf of spirit world. I don't feel I have to because I know that just because I don't understand something, doesn't mean it's not happening; that there are certain things we simply have to accept that we can never comprehend. I'll only understand it fully when I reach spirit world myself.

So, let's talk about that, shall we? Let's talk about spirit world. In other words, where will you go when you die?

Imagine a picture. This is earth plane. Now imagine somebody overlaying on it a piece of tracing paper. You can see through the tracing paper, clearly making out the image beneath, but the picture now has two layers. This second layer is spirit world; it co-exists with us, a different dimension, and in it are the souls of those who have passed over.

So, spirit world isn't 'up there' or 'down there'. I do talk about people being 'up in heaven' – and when I refer to heaven during readings and shows I'm talking about spirit world – but that's a form of shorthand; it's just a quick and easy way for people to understand the place in which spirits reside, like the way you look up when you talk to God, even though we know that he's everywhere, and that he fills the earth. Spirit world is the same – it's all around us. In many ways, we move within it.

Just as we can't give spirits the same desires and characteristics we have on earth, so it is that spirit world defies our mortal ideas of place or boundaries. Whatever you've seen in movies – in the representations of heaven you see in films such as, say, *Bruce Almighty* – it just isn't like that. It is not a *place*, with walls and doors and ceilings and a colour scheme. Instead, it is a field of potential; one that is inhabited by the souls of those who have passed over and who exist in a similar state to what I saw that first day in the hospital and have witnessed many times since: as a vapour, a breeze. That said, spirits can still take human form, and this is the state they usually adopt when they use me to pass messages to their loved ones on earth plane.

And that's what they love to do most, of course. When spirits first pass over they meet with their loved ones, who introduce them to the afterlife. There, they can move around quite freely – with the freedom of air – and what they do there is watch over their loved ones on earth.

Remember what I said: we all have a spirit who attends us. You have one right now, at your shoulder, watching over you. That spirit, by looking out for you, is serving a kind of apprenticeship. He or she is hoping to move towards Divinity.

Thirteen

At the right-hand side of God . . .

The way I believe it works is that there are three levels to life and death: level one is earth plane, level two is spirit world, then comes Divinity.

Most of us will go to spirit world. There, we earn our place in Divinity. Some, however, will go straight there – providing they have done wonderful things while on earth. Think of this and the likes of Mother Teresa or Gandhi spring to mind, people who have achieved great and good things, who no doubt go straight to Divinity. But don't worry, that doesn't exclude everyone else: your fast-track to Divinity might already have been decided, even if you're no saint.

How? Well, maybe you did something when you were little that you no longer have memories of. Say you gave a toy to another child who had nothing. Or perhaps you've said something to somebody that changed their life – without even knowing you'd done it. And doing that one tiny thing, years and years ago, has a kind of ripple effect. It may well have been an off-the-cuff remark you made: 'Oh, you look nice today!' Or: 'I really like that pair of jeans,' but it somehow lifted the recipient of the compliment, and because they were feeling a little better they did something which helped somebody else and the good turn was paid forward.

And so on and so on.

What I'm saying is, you may not even be aware that your actions have such incredible consequences – that they may create an opening for you in the top tier of the afterlife. So don't lose heart. Don't think, 'I haven't done anything, I'm no Mother Teresa,' because you may already have achieved your place. You may be *about* to achieve your place. In short, there's no iron rule. You'll only know when you get there. And, anyway, if you don't get straight there, don't worry, you're with the majority of other souls who will spend their apprenticeship in spirit world, looking over their loved ones, looking out for them, before they make the move upstairs, to the next level.

Now, what I'm saying here seems to suggest that everybody in spirit world is trying to do good deeds in order to get 'promoted' to Divinity, like scouts on Bob-a-Job week, but that's just my way of looking at things and, you know me, I like a bit of 'plain English'. I don't like dressing things up in mumbo jumbo. So what I'm giving you here is simply a way of looking at the structure of spirit world so we can all easily understand it. I cannot emphasize this enough: on the other side things are so, so different to our plane. Everything there exists purely as an energy. For instance, on earth plane we have to lug around this 'host' – the body – which plays such a big part of the huge mess we are in here, but which just isn't an issue in spirit world.

Think of it: vanity, greed, envy. These are all mortal, earth-plane weaknesses. A man sees a woman, he thinks, 'Phwoar.' He chats her up. She likes him back. They have an affair. There is a knock-on effect to those around them, a kind of dreadful fall-out – the ripple effect I was talking about earlier, except a negative version of it.

When you look at it like that, it is almost as though the body has the potential to poison the soul. It can't, actually – the soul is stronger than that – but that potential is there. The opposite, however, simply cannot exist. The soul cannot poison the body because the soul is never bad.

Oh, well, very, very rarely the soul is bad. But I'll come to that. Let's put it this way, though: a bad soul won't get to Divinity. It will never sit alongside the divine spirits, at the right-hand side of God.

Now you're thinking, *Hang on. God? She's saying we get to sit with God?*

Yes. I believe God is at the very summit in spirit world, at the head of Divinity and those divine spirits who sit with him – our great-great grandfathers and great-great grandmothers – somehow become part of his energy and by doing that have gained something – an extra knowledge.

I think that spirits who reach Divinity remain in the same form but have more freedom of movement than their counterparts in spirit world, and I think that those souls in Divinity have some kind of instant connection with earth plane; a hotline, if you like.

And that when they appear to those of us on earth plane, they appear as angels.

My belief in this has only been strengthened by my work, because I often give readings for people who are looked after by an angel, a divine spirit, and I've met people who describe meeting angels. They will talk about a ten-foot man or woman with wings. 'It saved my life,' they tell me. What's more, near-death experiences are often associated with angel sightings. This leads me to believe – and, again, it's one of those things I'm eager to discover when I do pass over – that the divine spirits, if they are angels, behave in an almost supervisory way: being so close to God, they do God's work. If those spirits in spirit world are the foot soldiers, then the angels are the generals.

Fourteen

All you need is . . .

Love, you see.

At a show, I got a man who came through, who wanted to speak to his wife, Nessy. She was in the audience and I said to her, 'I hope this isn't going to be too personal, love,' (sometimes, the things that come through you, wouldn't believe), 'but do you feel him in bed with you?'

The audience roared.

So did she, but I was right. It turned out she used to lie in bed at night and feel him with her – comforting her.

I had a message from him and all.

'Don't be afraid,' I told her. 'He whispers in your ear and kisses you, doesn't he?'

She nodded.

'Why are the eyes important? Is he kissing your eyes?'

'I used to kiss his eyelids,' she said, wiping tears from her cheeks.

'He loved that,' I said, getting another message from him. 'You must imagine you're kissing his eyelids,' I told her, passing it on. 'He wants you to imagine kissing his eyelids.'

She smiled. 'I'll do that.'

'Is there anyone called Patty?' I asked.

'That's his name,' she said, 'that's what we called him.'

'Well, he's here, touching your hair, rubbing your head.'

He mentioned lighting candles and burning incense. She did that, she told me. He asked me to make sure she continued. These, I knew, were two people who had been very much in love and still were – even though he had passed.

'His essence is joined to your essence,' I told her, and never have I believed it more. I say this during my show and I can't stress it enough here, but the magnetic pull in spirit world is one of pure love.

However, when I tell people this – how souls of loved ones are attracted to one another – I have worried people who say to me, 'But I've loved more than one person on earth plane – what will happen when I reach the other side? Who will my spirit join?'

My answer is always the same. The love that exists in spirit world is so different to that which we experience on earth plane. As human beings, our love is exclusive. If it's the right one, we only love that one person. However, when we die our love becomes *inclusive*. So, in other words, you might have four wives or four husbands, all of whom you loved differently. On earth plane there is no way that you could possibly consolidate all four of those loves – certainly not in most cultures anyway. In spirit world, things are different. All of these spirits can co-mingle because love is inclusive; there's no such thing as jealousy.

The reason for that is because the soul is far more sophisticated when it reaches the other side; it achieves a state where it can manage its emotions more successfully.

I'll give you an example. I did a reading for a lady in America who was having a hard time with her family.

It was as though something had skipped a generation. This lady, let's call her Jane, was a humanitarian, very caring, compassionate, artistic and creative. However, she never felt supported in her artistic endeavours by her family, especially her father, who was more right-wing in his views. Instinctively, she felt an affinity with her grandfather, who had passed over. In life, he had been active in human rights and it was to him she was drawn, so when she came to see me it was natural that it should be her grandfather she wanted to contact.

I don't pretend to understand the ins and outs of her family life, but there was a system in her family where grandparents were 'allocated' two grandchildren. And if that seems strange to you, well, it didn't make a lot of sense to me either, but this is the way it was for Jane, and it was particularly upsetting for her because the grandfather to whom she felt so close was not the grandparent allocated to her under the system (sounds like a very cockamamie system to me, but there you go). Again, this was another reason she was so keen to make contact with him. I think she thought it was a bit of a weirdo system as well, because it meant that her grandfather was kept separate from her. The way it seemed to me, it was as though this caring, artistic grandfather was somehow the glue that had kept them together, and since he'd passed over the individual members of the family were having problems relating to one another.

Anyway, I was able to make contact with the grandfather for Jane, and it was an amazing moment for her.

He was with her, he assured her. He was always with her.

'It's as though he's here with me now,' she said afterwards. 'I feel as if I have a guardian angel in spirit.'

Ironically, she told me she wasn't 'an angel person'.

All of a sudden, though, she felt connected to him. It was as if he were in the room with us. As though he stood behind Jane with a comforting hand on her shoulder, offering her the support her earth plane family could not or would not give her.

'There's so much friction with my dad,' she had told me, sniffling. 'He's very right wing and I'm very left wing and we have these awful arguments. My dad always says that military solutions are the best solutions and that's exactly the opposite to what I believe. It's exactly the opposite to what my grandfather would have believed.'

She was hurting. Hurting because she didn't feel there was anybody behind her to support her; nobody at her side, to give her comfort and support; nobody there for her.

Knowing her grandfather was there, knowing her grandfather cared about her beliefs and her artistic aspirations, gave her so much comfort.

They were able to pass messages to one another through me. Jane's grandfather expressed sadness that his relationship with her wasn't able to develop while he was on earth plane because of this strange allocation system. Again, this brought a smile to Jane's face. Simply knowing this – knowing that her grandfather had regrets about their relationship during his life – was something that allowed her to move on from the hurt caused.

She felt his presence from the spirit world and it redressed the balance, gave her support and possibly inspiration, the strength to hold on to her humanitarian views and not to let them wilt in the face of her father's more right-wing ideals.

Now, I'm not being all political about this. It could have been the other way round. She could have had right-wing views; he could have had left-wing views. It's just that stifling the way somebody feels about something is not right. When all is said and done, Jane was being repressed as a human being on earth plane. She looked to the spirit world to provide her with an avenue of expression, and it came through for her.

This is why I think of us on earth plane as being immature souls; that when we move across to spirit world, we grow.

I see life on earth plane as being the first step in a journey of the soul. This is the stage during which the soul begins to grow. It is still quite a childlike, immature entity. Just as a child is reluctant to share his or her toys, but realizes when he or she grows up the benefits of sharing, so the soul learns about the ways of love. The transition from earth plane into spirit world represents the dawn of a great maturity for the soul.

So you see, I tend to think of the soul as being our calming, civilizing centre. I actually think we would be quite barbaric without the soul. You hear people talk of other people as having 'no soul'. That's what they mean – that they lack a certain something that helps them love, and understand, and feel, and grow. It means they lack the very essence of what it is to be a human being.

We are wonderful things, we human beings, capable of such great kindness, acts of selflessness and incredible heart-stopping courage; all of this when the soul is so young. So just imagine what it is to be a soul on the other side of that transition — a more mature spirit. Only then do you begin to realize how wonderful the soul can be; how far beyond our capabilities to understand them they must be. They so completely defy description and understanding; as human beings we simply have not evolved the facilities to cast the soul into words.

The soul is a feeling and an essence. It is love. And have you ever tried to describe love? Hard, isn't it?

Fifteen

Caring from the other side

Let me give you another example of that spirit love in action. One night at a show I was doing a reading for a woman and speaking to her husband, who was in spirit.

'Tell her the back door is rattling,' I was told.

'Why is he telling me to tell you that the back door's rattling?' I said.

She shook her head, obviously confused.

He was most insistent, the husband.

'Tell her the back door's rattling,' he told me, and I passed the message on to her.

She was still shaking her head, and I could see people around her shifting uncomfortably in their seats. At times like that I always get this horrible feeling that I'm delivering the wrong message to the wrong person. It can so easily happen. Remember what I was saying about the radio?

Often I have to plough on and hope that the penny will drop, or that I will eventually be directed to the right person.

Fortunately, this was one of those situations where I had it right. It was indeed a penny-dropping moment, because all of a sudden her hand flew to her mouth and I could see that she knew exactly what I was talking about.

'What is it, darling?' I said. 'You know, don't you?' I said, because she was nodding.

Nodding still, she said, 'I've lost the back door key.'

Of course, that was it. *Hallelujah*. She had lost the back door key and wasn't able to lock up. Now, I don't want to make any wild assumptions about this lady, but if she's anything like me she's probably a bit ditzy or absent-minded and I think hubby was still looking out for her. The picture I had was of her still-devoted husband on the other side, in the afterlife, probably tutting lovingly, thinking, 'She hasn't locked the back door. Anybody could walk in off the street.' That's what John would do. I know it.

I must say, what I think is lovely is how spirits will assemble at shows, ready to give messages to their loved ones. Among their many 'talents' is the fact that they know we're going to be in places before even we do.

I'll give you another example. Not long ago, at a show, I was speaking to someone who had killed herself. I went to a woman in the audience, and the spirit gave me a name.

'Who's Babs?' I asked.

'That's me,' she said.

Well, of course, there was a gasp from the audience. It's nice to be able to get a name on the first go; sometimes they can come out a bit garbled. The spirit told me she was glad she was there.

'She says you almost didn't come.'

Spot on. She nodded her head. 'That's true,' she said.

They know, you see. How do they do that? I think there's a kind of omniscience involved, an ability to oversee events on earth plain, at least those pertaining to your loved ones.

The way I've always seen it is a bit like a train track. (Bear with me, you'll find I'm full of little theories, and this is one of them.)

Because spirit world is this place of energy, it's not governed by earth laws of physics, or gravity, or – most importantly – time. As spirits are free of body and mind, they exist in a state of complete freedom, and I often wonder how they must feel when they look upon us from the spirit world. Do they feel sorry for us? To them, we must look as though we're walking around in leg irons, bound by all this boring earth-plane physics while they fly and swoop and soar, all-being and all-seeing.

Which, of course, means being able to see into the future as well as the past, which is where my train comparison comes in.

Imagine a train racing along a track. We on earth plane are on that train. We can see behind us and the immediate future only. But now imagine you're in spirit, and you exist in this place that is around and above earth plane, so you are able to rise high, high above the train, and look down upon its progress. And that way you can see what lies behind the train, but also, far, far in front of it. If there's an obstacle on the track – a tree, say – then you can see it way before the passengers on the train.

Of course, this makes it sound as though spirit can see with complete clarity, and then communicate the vision with the same clarity. Which they can't. What I have dis-covered over the years is that the lines of communication are never crystal clear. This is why I can be wrong or I can misinterpret information and it's why names can often be jumbled. I think a lot depends on how recently the spirit passed over, and on the urgency of their message. What I find is that recent spirits not only stick like glue to their loved ones on earth plane, but they also have better clarity of message. The same goes for the importance of their message. That spirit in Blackburn, for instance, had something so important to say that he came through loud and clear. Talking of which, you might ask about his reason for being there. Doesn't that make a mockery of my belief that spirits appear to help those on earth plane? Was his behaviour really motivated by love?

Yes, I think so, absolutely. He was on some kind of quest, that one. I like to think that he'd deliberately chosen his moment and chosen it well – and he realized that by speaking to the girl in front of all those people it might help to shame her into going to the police. I certainly hope it did anyway.

Either way, his reason for being there was for love, for comfort and for some kind of closure. Not something relatively petty like revenge, or some idea of justice. Justice and revenge are earth-plane concepts. They don't have them in spirit world.

People find this difficult to understand. They think some spirits must feel agitated, or a sense of injustice if they believe they've been taken from the earth plane too soon.

'Come on, Sally,' people say. 'What about people who die in car accidents caused by people on their mobile phones? Seemingly senseless, easily avoidable deaths? Surely they must be seething on the other side?'

No, they're not. For a number of reasons, really, but one of the main ones being that when we pass over our spirits make an important discovery regarding death.

We find out that it was our destiny to die that day; we achieve the understanding that, however we die, whether we are murdered or whether it's suicide, it was just another way of making the transition to the afterlife.

This means that spirits are far less concerned about the quality of death than they are about the quality of life for those they love on earth plane. So, for example, I often get spirits asking me to deliver messages to their loved ones about smoking or drinking, or their lifestyle choices, even though they know it doesn't make a blind bit of difference: when it's your time, it's your time.

I suppose that at the end of the day they just want us to be happy, and certainly if I was in spirit and saw that one of my grandchildren had turned to drugs, say, I would want them to stop. The thought of one of my grand-children behaving like 'Dave', the ex-boy-band member I met on the set of *Star Psychic*, well, it's just too horrible to bear; of course I would want to prevent it.

When you look at it like that, God, aren't we lucky to have these beautiful, benign forces looking out for us? Don't we have to be so thankful that there is a place in the universe for all this love?

Sixteen

Truly free spirits

I've been asked before if I see spirits around people all of the time. As I'm strolling down the street, do I see other pedestrians walking along with souls bobbing around them like balloons they've just won at a fairground?

The answer is *yes* and *no*.

I could, if I was open, but let's face it, I wouldn't be open walking down the street; I'd go mad if I was. Plus, I *usually* have to be invited. So if I'm in a situation where I'm doing a show or a reading at home, then the invitation is there, but walking down the street it's not. Which is not to say I don't see ghosts when I'm out and about: I do. They always take me by surprise, though.

As regards seeing spirits, what I tend to find happens is that if I'm open, spirits will move from their loved one over to me. It's a bit like if you walk into a room full of dogs with a handful of dog biscuits, you could expect to suddenly be mobbed by dogs. And with apologies to spirit world, but it's a bit like that for me; I'm a medium, I'm their portal back to earth plane. In other words, I have what they want: the ability to talk to both sides at the same time, and they all have messages they want to pass on.

Then again, they can whoosh and fly off. Sometimes

I can be talking to a client or somebody at a show, and I'll say, 'Oh, it's pulling back. It's as though it's on wheels.' And that's it. The spirit is gone.

But the funny thing is, I often think that the spirit somehow acts as some kind of link between me and the sitter, and I have had people say as much to me after a reading or a show: 'Do you know what? I felt it too.'

The other day during a show, I was talking to a lady whose father was in spirit and standing with me on stage. 'Guess what?' I said. 'Your dad just touched my shoulder.'

She said, 'Yes, Sally, I felt it too.'

How? I'm standing on the stage. Health and safety, you know – I'm not allowed to leave that stage. She was in the circle if I remember rightly, 100 feet away from where I was standing, and yet she still felt that *very same touch on the shoulder.*

That's because of the link, the bond, and I find that absolutely fascinating, the way spirits are able to manifest themselves in so many different ways.

It's interesting that souls are still able to 'touch' like that, for I've certainly had people argue with me about the passage of souls. They say how awful it must be to have to give up your body. After all, the body can afford you so many pleasures; the idea of being free of the body just isn't that attractive.

'What are you going on about, Sally? How can it be *better* to be in spirit? I want my body.'

Well, yes, I can see that point of view, certainly. But think of the limitations of the body. I'm sorry, there's no nice way of saying this, but the body is in a state of decay. It ages, it gradually stops working. Even when it is working properly, it is very prone to malfunction. It's very delicate, fragile. It can be strong, but it can also be quite weak.

Spirits just don't have this problem, and time and time again, I speak to those in spirit who are overjoyed to finally be rid of the body, something they come to think of as an encumbrance.

Take a lady I had on stage not long ago. She was calling out a name. When I relayed it, it prompted a shout of recognition from further back in the auditorium and the microphone went to three ladies who sat together, who turned out to be sisters.

The lady in spirit seemed to have died from something in the neck area. I put my hand to my throat because I could feel something there.

'Why do I feel something at my throat?' I said. 'She didn't cut her throat, did she?'

'No,' came the reply from the lady in the audience. 'She had motor neurone disease and she couldn't speak.'

The lady in spirit was telling me that she was fine now; there was no more disease; that she was so much happier now she was free of it.

'"Look," she's telling me, "I can move my fingers now."'

The ladies were all in tears by this point.

Now don't tell me that spirit world doesn't have a sense of humour, because you'll never guess what the next message was ...

'She says, "I can pass wind at last!"'

Well, you can imagine. The audience was in hysterics. The three ladies, too.

'She's all right now,' I added, 'she's in a lovely place. She loves it there.'

'So she's not cross?' said one of the sisters.

'Oh no,' I said, 'she's happy, she can pass wind.'

Which was funny – but it was also a humorous way of saying something really quite profound about her journey to the other side. She was free.

How amazing is that? Think about it. How wonderful would that be, to be a spirit? I mean, we talk about such things as free spirits, but I really and truly believe that this is exactly what happens on the other side, this is what we become: *free spirits*.

I wouldn't go so far as to say that our bodies are jailers of the soul, though there are those who believe that. Just that they are vessels – quite basic, rudimentary, primitive vessels – in which the soul is carried before it is truly born. Perhaps what I'm talking about isn't life after death, because it's not life as we know it. Instead, it is something more evolved. I keep on saying this, but I truly believe that spirit world, far from representing death as being a negative thing, is actually the next step for us. It is the next, higher place. The destination for our souls.

Seventeen

Seeing ghosts

I am by no means the only method of communicating
with those on earth plane, just the most direct. If they
want to make themselves known, then they will.

I'll talk about reading the signs later, but if you're open
to communicating with loved ones who have passed
over, my first advice would be to pay special attention to
important dates. I can guarantee that if somebody says
to me, 'It's really weird. I saw my dad and he's been dead
forty years,' I'll say to them, 'Really? What day was it?'
And they'll go, 'Oh my God, that was his birthday.'

Look out for signs on other dates, too. The anniversary of the death, or special days they loved: Christmas,
Easter or other special days – it could even be the day
they went on a much-treasured holiday, for example.

Dates are very, very important in our dealings with
spirit world. It's not because spirits cling on to dates
the way we do on earth plane. They don't. After all, they're
energy, gas, light; believe you me, they don't have
calendars in spirit world.

It's because on earth plane – possibly subconsciously –
we project some kind of longing to communicate with
our loved ones that reaches across the two worlds; that

increases the magnetic attraction between spirit world and earth plane.

When we miss them most, in other words.

And it's the same with places.

Something happened recently where I had a man in spirit and I could see a cooker. His wife was in the audience and I told her what I could see.

She shook her head.

'It's an enormous cooker,' I pushed.

'No,' she said, still shaking her head, looking confused. It was one of those situations where I could tell she wanted to help me; she wanted to see the significance of an enormous cooker, but it just wasn't there.

As I've said, I get this a lot and the only thing to do in a situation like that is press on and hope that something will begin to make sense. It can get a bit nerve-wracking at times, to be honest.

'Not in a restaurant?' I said to her. 'There isn't a connection with a big cooker in a restaurant?'

Still she was shaking her head.

Then it came to me. Or, rather, it was given to me.

'He bought a cooker,' I exclaimed. 'Did he buy you a cooker, a big cooker?'

Now she was nodding her head. Yes, she'd remembered, he'd been to a specialist shop and bought one of those huge catering ovens, the kind you get in restaurants, like a range, but he'd had it installed in the house. She was blown away.

'It's still there,' she said.

'I know,' I said to her, 'he's telling me about it. And do you know something else?'

She shook her head.

'That's where his energy is,' I said. 'If you ever want to feel him, just go and fry an egg.'

The audience was laughing a little, and I admit it sounded funny, but it was the absolute truth.

It turned out that he had loved to cook and entertain, and was happiest preparing a meal. To find him, she only needed to go to that huge cooker in their kitchen, and he would be there.

'Stand there and think of him and he'll be there,' I told her. 'He'll have his hand on the pan, because that's what I'm seeing, his hand on the pan at the stove.'

What I'm saying is that if you lose someone and, say, they loved to go for walks, or had a favourite place, perhaps a beloved chair, or a seat in the back garden, then go to it. Their spirit will be invested in that place. We always leave something behind – we leave an energy behind.

Now, what about spirits who stay in one place? I'm talking about hauntings.

In spirit world, just as on earth plane, spirits need a sense of closure, so it is not unusual to stay in a place most associated with whatever is troubling them. I don't think they stay exclusively in this place, I really don't. I think that a haunting, if you want to call it that, applies really to a spirit revisiting that place on earth plane often, rather than being trapped there.

I realize, of course, that spirits do sometimes become trapped in a place, like a house – I have had to have a spirit exorcised from a house myself because it was making a nuisance of itself – but I think spirits like that are probably the exceptions rather than the rule.

That said, I've got some stories about badly behaved spirits.

Eighteen

Haunted

I have a friend who is based in the north of England. He is a lovely man, Shaun. He and his wife, Nancy, and their little boy, James, who is very autistic, live in a beautiful old stone farmhouse in a remote area very famous for its witches.

As you can imagine, I was most intrigued by this so I was dying to visit his house. Rather cheekily of me, I invited us over one weekend when I was in the north of England doing some shows.

'Oh, Sally, we'd love it,' said Shaun, luckily, because I had my heart set on it!

I must just tell you about his wife, Nancy. She's the loveliest woman but, I'm sure neither of them will mind me saying, completely batty.

Nancy has a crow. No joke, she has a pet crow that she rescued, which lives in their kitchen. She says it talks to her and, when she goes out walking, it accompanies her. You know what? I think she's a bit of a witch herself, Nancy, in the nicest possible sense. A witch without even knowing it. She reminds me a lot of Nanny Gladys.

To be honest, Shaun's just as off-the-wall. They make a perfect couple, in other words.

John and I toddled along to the house. We were there

for about an hour and had had a cup of tea and a natter in the kitchen, before − me having no doubt dropped a whole load of hints − we were given the grand tour of this house.

We went up to the first-floor landing and Nancy showed me a cubbyhole. It was slightly raised, like a secret place that needed a ladder to reach it. Perhaps it had once been a priest hole. At the far end of the space was a window, which was not visible from the outside; it had been bricked over.

'We find toys in there,' said Nancy, suddenly very serious. 'Just the odd thing, like an old teddy we found in there once, and a dolly that Shaun came across. We honestly have no idea where they come from.'

I looked into the cubbyhole and immediately felt something, like a chill. Descending the ladder, I found myself alone on the first-floor landing. Nancy and John had gone on ahead and, all of a sudden, I felt very, very frightened indeed.

I'm not usually one for feeling frightened. In my job, you can't really afford to be scared of the unknown. Wouldn't be much of a medium, would I, if I was getting goosebumps every time I sensed a spirit?

Yet here I was, and I was getting goosebumps. Something about this corridor had unnerved me. There was something dark here, something unknown.

I have, in the past, encountered malevolent spirits, and as I trotted up behind John and Nancy, I wondered: was there a bad soul in this house?

Now we came to a bedroom door and Nancy paused, one hand on the doorknob. She turned to John and me.

'This is James's room,' she said. 'He doesn't speak. By all means talk to him, in fact, please do, but he won't react. I just wanted you to know. It's not like he's being rude or anything, he just never speaks.'

She knocked softly before entering, and we stepped inside, me glad to get off the landing, where the unsettling feeling was bearing down on me as though it had physical form: a dark, slippery mass I was very happy to escape.

As we stepped inside the bedroom, James stood from where he had been sitting in the centre of his room and launched himself over to me, quite taking me by surprise, wrapping his arms around my legs and giving me a great big hug.

'Alison,' he said, 'Ally, at last you've come.'

Nancy's eyes were wide. Not only did James never speak, she told me later, but he wasn't given to displays of affection either. Yet here he was – as soon as I'd walked in the room he'd called me Ally and rushed over to give me a hug.

'I knew you were coming, Alison, I knew you were coming,' he said excitedly, bouncing up and down slightly.

I was petrified all over again. I knew that when James spoke to me he was talking to someone else – when he looked at me he was looking at someone else.

'You're Sally,' said Nancy to me, still in shock, I suppose, at James's unexpected outburst.

'I know,' I almost laughed, 'I know I'm Sally.' It would have been funny – it *might* have been funny in different circumstances – if it hadn't been for the fact that James never spoke, that he was calling me by another woman's name, that I knew when he spoke to me he was speaking to someone else.

Out on the landing I had sensed the presence of something very unwelcome in the house. A spirit. A restless soul. A spirit called Alison, perhaps? Who placed dollies in the secret cubbyhole?

'I'm Sally,' I told him, smiling, trying to keep the atmosphere as light as possible.

'No, no, you're Ally. They call you Ally, you're Alison. You remember me?'

'No, darling, I'm Sally,' I told him, as gently as possible.

'I can't believe this,' said Nancy. 'He goes to a special school and he has carers there that he hasn't spoken to in four or five years. This is incredible.'

He was rubbing my arm. In his eyes was a contented, faraway look that I found quite disconcerting.

I bent slightly to look at him. 'Do you know me, James?' I said.

He held my gaze. 'Yes, of course I know you. Of course I know you, Alison.'

He did. He knew me, all right. But it was somebody else he was looking at.

He wouldn't have it. In the end, we had to simply accept that, in James's eyes, I was this Alison and I had come back, and we left him to it in his bedroom, quite happy in our wake.

When we left that day, I said to John, 'That child is open. James has a gift; he can see things, but I tell you what – that house is not right for him. It's like Waldemar Avenue, the bad ghost at Waldemar Avenue, except that this house has one spirit, and I really don't think it's a welcoming one. I think it means somebody harm. I think that James is worse because he's living in the house.'

We talked about it a lot, and I spoke to Shaun on the phone, to check whether there had been any other incidences before or since.

There hadn't, it seemed, so I decided to keep my fears to myself. Was there any point in scaring this poor family rigid? They already had enough on their plate. I came to the conclusion that there was something about my presence in the house that had acted as a catalyst for the sudden spirit activity. It was the only explanation that made any sense.

Then, about six months later, I was back in the area, doing more shows, and I went to see them. Over a cup of tea, Shaun said to me, 'You know what, Sal? We're thinking of selling the house.'

I suppressed a cold shiver. 'Really?' I said, keeping my voice neutral. 'Why is that? It's so lovely and you've done so much to it and you're so happy here.'

'Well, it's funny,' he said. 'I don't think you picked it up when you were here last, but we think there is something – a spirit – on the first floor, maybe in James's bedroom. It seems to make James a bit manic.'

Hadn't picked it up, eh? I thought, but didn't say. I certainly picked it up all right.

It makes perfect sense to me that James would be more open to activity in the spirit world than his parents, for all sorts of reasons. His autism, for a start. Plus the fact that he was so young. I'll go into this in greater detail later, but it's all wrapped up in my theory of the valve. (No, don't laugh, you're going to like it.)

What I do know, though, is that there was a spirit in that house and it was hanging around, and as I stood on the landing that first afternoon I knew that it wanted to appear to me. I don't know whether it wanted to take on physical form and show itself, I had no idea; I stayed closed. Resolutely, I refused to open to the spirit. It was almost as though I could feel a bulge as it tried to push through, so desperate was it to make contact.

Now, that was me. I am able to open and close at will; I'm very lucky and I have been doing what I do for years and years. What scared me was that James had some definite ability but without being able to open and close. He was always open as far as spirit world was concerned and within reach of a potentially very nasty spirit indeed.

I wondered then whether I should suggest an exorcist. Years and years ago I had an exorcism performed at a house in which I lived with John and the kids. It was to deal with the spirit of a woman called Mrs Walters, as she was, quite frankly, making a real nuisance of herself, opening and shutting doors, slamming windows and suchlike.

It goes against my core beliefs to have an exorcism, because my feelings about troublesome spirits is not that they are trapped down here and want to be in heaven, or even that they have some unfinished business and they are trying to attract the attention of those of us on earth plane; I certainly don't buy the theories you see put forward in films, such as the *Amityville Horror*, where it seems as though the house is trying to frighten away its new occupants. I just don't believe any of that stuff at all. No, when I hear about a spirit misbehaving, I immediately think of a spirit that needs listening to, and nine times out of ten I might well be the one to listen to it.

Saying that though, there are obviously exceptions to the rule. The spirit of Mrs Walters that I had exorcised, for a start. I'm afraid she had to go for one reason: she was scaring the children. It's as simple as that.

This spirit in Shaun and Nancy's house was another exception to my rule, this time because it unnerved me so much. Again, it's as simple as that. There was something so dark and frightening about this particular presence that I just did not want to engage with it. I was petrified that day, I can tell you. They put their house on the market shortly afterwards and sold it. I hope against hope that the new occupants aren't quite as open to spirit as my friends.

So, yes, there is such a thing as a malevolent spirit, they are just very rare. Those that *are* malevolent, though, are different. That kind of spirit I see as being more of an entity – a presence, but an evil one.

Let me tell you another story. We have some friends who lived in a very famous house down south. I must protect the identity of the people involved, so I cannot name them or their house. I'm afraid you're just going to have to trust me on this: it was a very famous house. Situated on a clifftop on the coast, it was a perfect place to visit for a weekend, and so it was that John and I found ourselves invited.

Our bedroom was at the top of the house and was a beautiful room. It had a lovely, warm feeling to it, really cosy.

We were asleep one night and I heard somebody enter the room.

Our hosts had grown-up children who lived in the house. Indeed, it was one of their daughters' bedrooms that we were using for the night. Laura was staying at her boyfriend's house so I thought, when I heard the door go, that she must have returned to fetch something.

Stupid, really, it was the early hours of the morning. But you know how it goes sometimes? You just have this sleepy thought that somehow makes sense in the early hours. So I lay there, pretending to be in the land of nod, letting Laura fetch whatever it was she had come for.

Then came a voice, saying, 'Oh, sorry.' A woman's voice. Very distinctive. Posh.

Still pretending to be asleep, I didn't respond, thinking, *I'll just let her get on with it.*

Then I felt something.

It was a man's hand – well, it certainly felt like a man's hand – on my shoulder, grasping it. For a moment or so I felt a hand try to move me, as though trying to tip me over on to my side. And there was, just for those few seconds, a minor tussle between us, as my brain struggled to make sense of what was happening and failed to come up with any kind of rational answer.

Next the hand grabbed my boob.

When something like that happens, something so completely bizarre, the mind struggles to comprehend. It reaches for answers and cannot find them. It's funny, because I encounter this very phenomenon in my work all of the time, with cynics and sceptics who refuse to believe, even when the evidence is right there before their eyes. Because they have no answer, they flounder. Because they cannot explain the inexplicable, they simply refuse to believe it.

Which was what happened to me, that night. Or just for those few moments, at least. I felt the hands on me. I could feel the physical pressure, almost like a pain, and my mind was skipping through the possibilities. It wasn't Laura, it wasn't John, it wasn't our host. Then who was it?

Who was it?

At last, after what felt like minutes but was probably only half a second or so, I broke free of the mental grip and screamed, sitting up at the same time, pulling the sheets to my chest, feeling somehow ... violated.

Beside me, John was suddenly wide awake. 'What's wrong, love?' he said, eyes wide.

'It was a man,' I shrieked, 'a man. He was grabbing me and he was trying to push my shoulder. He was rubbing my chest.'

'You bloody what?' said John, shooting out of bed, fumbling for the bedside lamp and flooding the place with light. The bedroom was empty, nobody else there apart from John and me.

John was looking at me now, a strange look.

'I didn't imagine it, John, I promise. There was a man in here and he grabbed me. He was ... rubbing me. You've got to believe me, love.'

He dropped to the bed beside me, saying, 'Of course I believe you, Sally.' He grinned. 'Thousands wouldn't, but living with you, there's not a lot I don't believe, to be quite honest.'

You couldn't really ask for more than that in the middle of the night, could you? Someone there to protect you, to listen to you, to *believe* you.

I have to say I didn't get much sleep after that, though. The house was very old and with it came the sorts of noises you would expect with age. Cracks, creaks, things literally going bump in the night. No, I have to say I hardly got a wink after that.

The next morning we were at the table and I told our host, Miriam, who was making breakfast.

'How did you sleep?' she said, cracking eggs, wiping her hands on a pinny.

'Well, as a matter of fact I didn't sleep very well at all,' I said.

'Oh no, what was the matter? Was it the pillows?' she said.

'You're going to think I'm mad . . . but I thought Laura came into the room.'

'Oh no, she's staying at her boyfriend's house . . .'

'Well, I know that,' I said, 'but this woman walked in and said, "Oh, sorry."' I did an impression of the voice I had heard.

She stopped what she was doing. One hand held the bowl, and in the other a fork, poised to begin whisking the eggs.

'What did you say?'

'That I heard a voice, and it said, "Oh, sorry."'

Still she didn't move. 'No, but say it exactly as you did before. Use the voice you used before. The posh voice.'

I did it, exactly as I had heard the previous night.

Miriam placed the fork on the worktop. She turned to

face me, crossing her arms over her chest, face serious.

'It sounds like the same voice,' she said.

'The same voice?' I said.

'Yes,' she said. 'Not long after we moved in I heard a voice exactly like that. You know the glass panelling at the bottom of the staircase?'

I did. Beautiful, mahogany staircase they had, and at the bottom there was, as she said, some glass panelling.

'Well, I was cleaning it one day and I felt that a woman was standing next to me. It was just an impression I had of somebody standing by my side. Then, all of a sudden, I heard the voice. She said, "I do that, too."'

It was the same voice. Miriam and I were doing an impersonation of the same voice.

'Oh my God, Miriam, that's unbelievable. Now you're going to think I'm going mad – certainly John thinks I'm going round the twist – but shortly after I heard her voice I'm sure that there was a man in the room. He put his hands to me and pushed my shoulder down then he kind of rubbed . . .' I showed her what I meant.

'Oh, Sal, I'm so sorry. It sounds like you've met our ghost.'

'Your second ghost?'

'Yes, sounds like it. This one is a man and I think Claire has seen him. That's why she hates sleeping there.'

It turned out that their other daughter, Claire, had taken a different bedroom and had it converted into a flat because she hated using that room so much. Laura, well, she was so rarely at home these days it didn't seem to bother her.

'That's why Claire won't sleep there,' said Miriam. She

had made her flat in the old servants' quarters in the loft.

'Well, thanks a bunch for telling me,' I said, before we both burst out laughing.

That day we did some looking into the background of the house. It is such a famous house it wasn't really that difficult, to be honest.

What we found was that it had been used for smuggling. Miriam's theory – and I think she's right – is that the man in my room was a fisherman, a dead smuggler.

Crikey, I thought, *felt up by a randy fisherman ghost*. Doesn't bear thinking about, does it?

Miriam swears she's seen him wearing an old sou'wester and a cape, which conjures up a really creepy image. Apparently, he's known for groping women. That's what you might call his preference. To me, that's an example of a malevolent spirit because he knows exactly what he's doing and he's deliberately doing it to frighten people – women – which makes him fairly despicable in my view.

In my experience, though, it's rare for spirits to be up to no good. A little mischievous, perhaps – and I think they play as fast and loose with the truth in the afterlife as we sometimes do on earth plane – but hardly ever actually malicious. It goes back to what I've been saying about spirit world and how they are so motivated not by our earth-bound concerns, but by love.

Before you go thinking I'm some kind of hippy, though, I don't think it's all peace and love on the other side. Not every spirit has a soul brimming with love. There are such things as bad souls . . .

Nineteen

Bad souls

One of the questions I'm most frequently asked is: *What happens to bad people when they cross over to the other side?*

The answer is that they join spirit world, along with all the rest of the souls.

'Really?' comes the reply. 'Even if they've done very, very bad things?'

My answer to that is that truly bad souls are extremely rare indeed. The majority of souls are good. Instead, what you sometimes get is a good soul poisoned by the frailties of the human mind and body: greed, envy, avarice.

But these things have absolutely no currency in spirit world. There, a kind of equality is in operation and lines of good and bad are less easy to draw. It's more sophisticated than that and more subtle.

Do I think there is some kind of reckoning when you get there? Yes, I do. I don't believe there is some sort of panel that sits in judgement, but certainly we're asked to look back at our lives to see the mistakes that we made, as well as the good that we did.

When you think about it, it makes absolute sense. Remember, I see our time on earth plane almost as practice for our tenure in spirit world – all part of our training, part of our journey towards Divinity. And what do you do when you're training? You do dry runs, don't you? Very often you record yourself doing these practice sessions and you watch yourself to see where you went wrong and where you can improve. It's the best way to learn. Well, this is what happens when you reach spirit world.

I'll tell you what it's not, though: it's not 'this is right, this is wrong', the kind of rules you'll find in most religions, which, I have to be honest, I find quite frustrating, because religions are so *definite* about things; they don't have room for shades of grey; they don't accept that there may be degrees of right and wrong.

What I always say is that every murderer was once a child who wouldn't have hurt a fly. Perhaps those who are bad are not 'soulless' as some would like to say; instead their mistake is in not listening to their soul.

Now, this leads me on to something that I have another theory about. And I might get a bit of stick for this. But here goes nothing . . .

Twenty

My theory of heaven and hell

While I do believe that souls are corrupted by the mind and body, or the mind and body fail to listen to the soul, creating a corruption, I also know that there is occasionally such a thing as a bad soul.

There is, I am very sad to say, great evil in this world. You know the kind of thing I'm talking about: the Peter Sutcliffes and the Adolf Hitlers of this world; the Myra Hindleys. They don't stay in spirit world, and they certainly do not attain Divinity. My belief is that they are sent back down to earth plane – very quickly. Their souls are re-used.

Which means, what I am saying is . . . that earth plane is a kind of hell.

OK, perhaps that's a bit strong and I should say instead that it is purgatory, and even then it is, after all, a fairly benign form of purgatory. After all, the earth is a beautiful place. It is full of quite wondrous sights, miraculous achievements, a testament to the goodness of the human heart, and the last thing I want to suggest is that you're living in a 'hell', because I dearly hope you're not. I hope that your life is, like mine, full of great love and happiness.

However, it is a *form* of hell. Not because we are all

consumed by great fires of damnation; on the contrary, we're not. It is a hell compared to what follows. That is important – really important – to remember. However heavenly your life on earth plane, it is nothing compared to what spirit world has in store for your soul.

Unless, of course, you are in possession of a truly evil soul. It's my belief that people like Hitler – people who have committed dreadful atrocities like genocide and mass murder – I believe that when they die they are sent back.

As what?

Well, now, that's the $64,000 question, isn't it?

One thing I do believe is that it's not as another bad soul. I think there's more to the grand plan than a sort of endless cycle of punishment. I suppose what I hope is that these bad souls are somehow 'washed' along the way; that they are purged of their evil. I really hope this, most fervently. I have to hope that they are recycled in a way that is somehow beneficial to earth plane.

But it's not just bad souls that are recycled. Other souls are, too. I'm sorry if this is freaking you out a little. I really don't mean to do your head in. But I suppose your next question would be, 'If souls are somehow recycled from the spirit world back to earth planc, could I be a recycled soul?'

Which is an interesting question ... one I'm not sure I can answer in full. But remember what I was saying before, about how I think that I might be needed on earth plane even after I have passed over? If that is the case for me, then maybe it is also the case for other souls. There are certain people who I look at, especially children, and I think, 'That is an old soul.' Two of my grandchildren I look at and think, 'They've been here before.' In the grand scheme they are of more use to those of us on earth plane than they are to the spirits in spirit world.

So if earth plane is hell, then what about heaven?

There is no single definition of heaven. When we are in spirit world, we go to our *own* version of heaven. I know this, because when I talk to those who are in spirit I often see them in a lovely place, a place that I know corresponds to somewhere on earth plane that made them very, very happy indeed. They are in a 'happy place', you could say. Their very own little piece of heaven. Because just as earth plane represents hell, so the spirit world is heaven, and that heaven will change depending on . . . well, you.

I'll give you an example. Not so long ago a lady came to see me and I found myself talking to her husband, who was in spirit.

'He's in a room,' I said. 'I can see a rocking chair. There's a sofa on the other side of the room.'

'Oh my gosh,' she said, then told me that I had just described her husband's study, which is where he used to go, joking that he loved to get a little bit of peace and quiet there. She often used to find him asleep in the rocking chair, with a newspaper across his lap, or perhaps a copy of the latest Ian Rankin novel.

It is quite extraordinary, isn't it? This was his room – his very special, personal place. I have no doubt that he spent many, many happier moments with her, or with his children, on holiday, in the garden, or at birthday parties.

But there was something about this room that was very personal to him. It was where he went in order to access an inner calm. And what do you know? There in spirit world he has found that place. In the afterlife we are allowed to surround ourselves with the things that made our life special. And when we are happy – well, it's infectious, isn't it? That happiness affects other people's lives. How else are spirits supposed to help those of us on earth plane? How can they do that if they are not happy? When you think about it, it makes perfect sense that in order for somebody to do their job to their best ability they should be content. Him upstairs, well he creates exactly that environment for his workers. Pretty clever when you think about it. Makes good business sense, I suppose!

I think that spirit world is completely wonderful, warm place, where we are totally safe. Yes, if I were to describe the afterlife in one word, it would be that: safe.

Imagine being in a place where you know you are loved so much. That's what it's like.

The closest thing I can imagine on earth plane is the joy that you experience when you look at your children and you feel such love that it completely defies description, and it's a love that flowers and flourishes inside you, almost bursting from within you, so that it seems to rise up your throat, like it wants to whoosh from your mouth. That's what it's like.

As I've already said, my gut instinct is that I will come back to earth plane in order to continue my work – but if I do get the chance to stay, heaven for me will be sitting on a beach. I can picture it. There are very few people around and I can hear the water. My kids are OK, everyone is healthy and I'm drifting off to sleep ...

That for me is heaven on earth, and that for me is what lies in store on the other side.

And isn't that a lovely thing to know? Not just for yourself, but for your loved ones, too. It's nice to know that if you lose somebody you love they are going to a far, far better place.

However, even armed with that knowledge, the process of bereavement will always be very, very painful indeed. I want to go into that in a bit more detail.

Twenty-one

Beginning to grieve

When I was just starting out I did a big event at Kingston University, one of those where I would turn up and do readings for an audience, similar to my shows now, but on a much smaller scale. It was there that I did a reading for a boy named Johnny.

Johnny was there with his girlfriend, who explained to me that he had trouble speaking – a symptom he had developed since the tragic death of his mother and his stepfather.

Johnny had to have a can of drink with him at all times; he couldn't swallow without it. Somehow, his grief had become an actual lump in his throat that he could not swallow. It had come on from the moment he heard about his mother and his stepfather's death. His inability to talk was a physical manifestation of grief.

His parents were in spirit with him and when I spoke to them it turned out they had both been killed in the Zeebrugge disaster. I was able to give Johnny details of their death, as well as pass messages to him, then saw him again afterwards for further sessions. Johnny was able to overcome this problem and these days he's fine. It was wonderful to be able to help him, but in return he did me a huge favour: he taught me a lot about the way grief can work on us. I saw that even though we think of it as having a psychological impact, the effects can be physical too, and very often in a specific part of the body intrinsically linked with my work: the throat area. I've since seen countless examples of the same symptoms – people going through the process of bereavement who say that they cannot swallow properly.

Why the throat? It's all to do with the soul because the throat and soul are so close together. Interlinked, almost. As a result, it's very common for bereavement-associated problems to be located in this area, and if you have just lost somebody – or know somebody who has – you should be very wary of this. Take care of that throat area and you will be helping to protect your soul. You need to, you really do. Grief can creep up on you, otherwise.

So much of my work involves reading the recently bereaved, and it's here that the counselling element of it is most apparent. I'm often asked how to define grief, usually by those still in shock from the death of a loved one; those who are still trying to make sense of their emotions.

For me, a definition of bereavement would be an ache, an ache of knowing that you're never going to see that person again – not in the physical body anyway. That's it in simplistic terms; it represents a time when a person is forced into feelings they have never had before. As you know, I see the soul as an essence of pure love, and it's easy to imagine that just as it reaches out to loved ones, it can also be easily bruised. This can be diagnosed as a form of stress, or a kind of drawn-out panic attack – a state triggered by a profound sense of loss. Your loved one is gone, in a very literal sense. The body is gone. And on earth plane we tend to see things very much in terms of 'the body'; we're conditioned to view ourselves and those around us as flesh and bone. Something to hold and touch and feel. When you're deprived of this, it's natural and understandable to go into panic mode. That is the start of bereavement.

There are different stages to it, though. You will most likely experience anger at first. Then there is sadness. Dreadful, dreadful, sadness. Then more anger and frustration. Why? What? Where? When? Couldn't I have done more? These are all the questions you will have. There is guilt involved; loneliness, sometimes; shame, perhaps.

In fact, virtually any negative emotion you can think of will at some point be associated with the process of grieving. And don't think all of this happens in any kind of logical or chronological order either, because it doesn't. It is simply down to the individual and how they cope; it will depend on the circumstances in which they lost their loved one. It will also depend on their own state of mind and situation.

One thing I do know is that there is no set pattern, and that grief can be very cruel, striking at the most random and unexpected moments. People think, 'I've had a couple of days of feeling a bit better,' and then they can be walking along the street or waiting at a bus stop, or sitting at traffic lights waiting for them to go green and suddenly, *bang*, it's there, a memory – a memory that comes flooding back.

And the next thing they know, they're in floods of

tears, bawling uncontrollably into shaking hands, traffic beeping around them. Total pain. Utter devastation.

What I try to impress on them at times like that is that it's a question of interpretation. It's like a radio signal that's indistinct and unlistenable. There's nothing wrong with the signal, it's all down to the radio. It just needs tuning. Try not to unscramble the signal as pain, or loss, or grief. Try to see it for what it is, which is spirit world sending you a message. A spirit saying, 'I'm still here. I'm still with you, darling.'

Is it really a message from spirit world, people often want to know?

Yes. Something I always tell people – clients, people who come to my shows – is that we are all the messengers. We are the radios. Sometimes we're tuned and sometimes we're not, which is why spirits can pop into your head and trigger memories.

I like to see spirits as a kind of force in waiting. We're not aware of them there, but one of the ways in which we access them is to look out for certain signposts, one of which can be memory. In other words, *spirits trigger memories*.

I've spoken before about how this can happen at certain times and places and later I'll talk about how you can develop your own psychic ability and be aware of the messages sent by spirit world. Suffice to say for the time being that because spirits are around us all of the time, that also means your loved ones are around you all of the time.

Even – especially, actually – those spirits who have recently passed over.

It's a very cheering thought, isn't it? What I find even more heartening is that those who have passed over will always, *always*, try to bring comfort to those they have left behind. They always want to help.

For example, at one show I got a lady called Pat who came through. She wanted to speak to an Eric, her husband, who was in the audience; we got a mic to him.

Pat gave me a message for Eric. 'I only get upset on birthdays,' she told me.

'She wants to be around you on your birthday,' I said to Eric. 'Now, there's someone in spirit with her called Harry. Do you know a Harry?'

He nodded.

'So she's not lonely.' Then something more came to me. 'Eric,' I said, 'did you recently have a sneezing fit or a nosebleed?'

'I had a nosebleed recently,' he confirmed, eyes shining.

'Pat's saying to me, "Don't blow your nose like that."'

He laughed. 'She always said that to me.'

Then came a lovely little exchange. Eric said, 'Sally, can I ask you something?'

'Yes, of course you can, darling.'

'Just last week, I had an experience, where . . .'

It came to me and I leapt in. 'I know what you're going to say,' I blurted. 'Crying. You saw her crying.'

'Yes,' he agreed, adding, 'I wanted to know why she was crying. Is she not happy where she is?'

'No, darling,' I said. 'She didn't think you were going to come tonight is all it is. She was worried you might not make it.'

It was lovely. Very rarely before have I had a sense of such great love between two people, and it was a great message to be able to deliver. I tend to think of myself as a pleaser – perhaps that's why I was chosen for this work – so the messages that give me the greatest satisfaction are those that bring greatest comfort and closure to people.

On the other hand, of course, are those that end badly and messily, and leave you with a nasty taste in the mouth . . .

Twenty-two

Pure evil ...

One of those nasty-taste-in-the-mouth episodes came when I was working abroad. I was in this particular country because I had a client I'd seen in the UK who offered to organize lots of readings for me there.

John and I were both in our late forties – kids left home – and we wanted to see a bit more of the world, so we thought, 'Well let's just go and have a look. What have we got to lose?'

So we went there, loved it – the weather, the people, just gorgeous – and I soon found myself with a large client base and doing very well. I missed home, of course. You do, don't you? And I missed my kids, too. But life was good.

What used to happen was, I would do the readings in people's homes. The idea was that I'd go along to a client's house, and he or she would invite seven or eight of their friends and I would do readings for them all. On this particular day I had come to the very last client, a lady, and as we started talking I had a sense of darkness. Not dark as in the absence of light. No, this was dark as in *evil*. Pure evil.

I looked at her. She returned my gaze. There was nothing about her to suggest she was different from anyone else I'd seen that day. Nothing about her you'd consider 'dark'.

'I'm sorry,' I said. 'This might sound like a bit of a weird question . . .'

'Yes,' she said, brow furrowing. Goodness, what on earth must she have been thinking? What was this crazy psychic about to say? On the other hand, perhaps she knew . . .

'Do you have an acquaintance who was murdered?'

Sometimes the words come out of my mouth before I even realize what I'm about to say. It's as though they bypass the normal processes. It's why I can say something like that and it takes me by surprise as much as it does her.

And it did – it did take her by surprise. Her hand flew to her mouth. 'Oh my God, yes, I do . . .' The blood seemed to drain from her face.

'Well,' I said, 'it's really odd, but the thing is – they don't have her body, do they?'

'No, they don't.'

I had an image in my head, a place that I tried to describe, only I wasn't doing a very good job, so in the end I thought maybe I could draw it. I said to her, 'Do you have a piece of paper or something?'

She had this tiny little diary that she pulled out of a bag and handed me a pen.

Now, though, I hesitated, not sure I could do it.

'Please try,' she pressed. 'I can show it to my husband. He's a policeman.'

Ah, so that was why it had come to me during the reading, that feeling of darkness. Suddenly it all made sense.

Without thinking, my hand guiding me, I drew what I thought was a shed.

'It's made out of what-d'you-call-it?' I said. 'You know . . . corrugated iron, that's it. And it's beside a road, a busy main road.'

I sketched some trees, the picture forming as those in the room craned to look over my shoulder. Now I found myself pointing to the corrugated iron shed, somehow knowing that, 'This area here is going to be a car park. It wasn't a car park when she was murdered but it's going to be . . . it's going to be a car park.'

The image in my head was growing in strength. I could smell the night, could hear the traffic, see the trees. It was like watching a movie, a thriller – a dark, dramatic thriller.

'She was taken into here,' I said, indicating the corrugated iron shed again. 'She was taken into here and killed.'

Then, somehow, I knew. I just knew. I looked at the policeman's wife, looked back at the piece of paper, the pen shaking slightly in my hand as I pointed to the picture.

Then I said, the words appearing in my head and leaving my lips before I even knew they were there: 'Put underground here.'

Those exact words. That was exactly what I said. *Put underground here.* Where it came from, that particular phrase, I don't know. A spirit? No doubt. A spirit, putting images and words into my head.

After I had finished my drawing and the policeman's wife had put it in her handbag, she explained about the case. A girl – we'll call her Fay Raeburn – had been murdered two years prior to my arrival in the city. There had been three murders in the area. Two of the bodies had been found, but not Fay's, even though she'd been the first to disappear. Police were linking all three but had no body with which to prove their theories. Fay had been a friend of hers at school, she told me, which must have been another reason the image had appeared to me, and so strongly as well.

I left the house shaken, trying to somehow forget the image of that terrible, horrible place. A place of darkness. A place of murder. Was she there? Was Fay in that shed? I couldn't be sure. But I thought so.

Twenty-three

Good cop, bad cop

It was hours later that the phone rang. It was quite late at night by now, so it was unusual to receive a call at that time.

'Hello,' said a male voice, a policeman.

How did I know he was a policeman? A psychic knowing? I'm not sure – I think he just had a policeman's voice.

After he'd introduced himself – his first name was Jason – he said, 'Can we come and collect you in the morning, Mrs Morgan? We'd really like to interview you. It's about the disappearance of Fay Raeburn . . .'

It's almost impossible not to feel a tiny little worm of paranoia slithering around in the pit of your stomach at a time like that. *We want to interview you.* There's something about that sentence that sounds so sinister. They didn't think, did they, that . . . No, of course not. How could they? From what I had discovered, these terrible, tragic events had taken place when I was on a different continent.

Even so, you can't help but worry at a time like that, and that night I lay awake fretting until, after what seemed like hours, I finally laid my worries to rest. *Oh, come on*, I told myself, *how on earth could they suspect me of wrongdoing? Don't be ridiculous, Sally.*

So by the time it got to actually meeting the police, I felt as though I would be OK. But I wasn't.

It was an interrogation. There's no other word for it. And I had never been so frightened in my life.

The next morning two detectives came to the door. One was Jason; the other Bruce. At first they were nice, introducing themselves and generally being very polite. They were all smiles, in fact. It turned out all this was for John's benefit. They obviously didn't want him kicking off and insisting on accompanying me. It worked. He stood by the door as I gave him a peck on the cheek and told him I'd see him later, setting off with my police escort.

However, when we reached the car Jason got into the driving seat, ushering me into the back seat. I stepped inside, expecting the second detective to sit next to his partner. Instead, Bruce sat next to me. At once, I felt uncomfortable. I'd seen enough films – I'd watched enough TV – to know that this wasn't quite right.

They suspect me, I thought, that worm of paranoia returning – with a few pals.

Then, *No, they can't. How could they?*

They suspect me.

Suddenly, it didn't feel like, 'Oh, we just want to have a quick word.' It felt like I was under arrest. It felt as though I was under suspicion.

Oh God, I thought. And you know what? My friends that morning had encouraged me to have a lawyer present and I'd pooh-poohed the idea. I'd dealt with my paranoia, remember. What would I need a lawyer for, I told my friends? They just wanted to talk. The idea was that they'd pick me up, then drive me to the office I was working from during my stay.

'We'll talk in the car,' I'd been told on the phone the night before, but it turned out to be small talk. Well, I say small talk. I mean 'small talk' in inverted commas, because they were using the journey to try to find out as much about me as possible – without it seeming that way. You can't blame them. I guess that's the way policemen work all over the world.

'How long have you been doing this?' they asked. 'Have you been in the country long? Have you travelled around at all? Met many people?'

A couple of sceptics, I knew instantly, simply from the way they were talking about my ability. Just my luck. There was something about the way they spoke to me.

'Well, you're scientists,' I said to them after one too many slightly sneering comments, 'you're men of science, it's hardly surprising that you don't believe in what I do.'

I may have been scared, but I wasn't going to let them know it. They continued to probe me for information, all the time as though we were having a friendly conversation.

Looking out of the car window, Bruce sitting next to me, I certainly wished I had taken my friends' advice. Perhaps I even wished I had kept my mouth shut about the shed I had seen. Until, finally, we arrived.

The office I was using was owned by a friend of mine, a lovely guy called Phil, who had a very busy, thriving business. At front of house was a reception area that my friend Grace worked in. Into it I came, flanked by my two new detective friends.

'Oh, Grace,' I said, greeting her. 'You'll never guess what? I saw a woman yesterday and I said something to her and apparently there's been a murder.'

'Murder?' said Grace, mouth dropping so far open I thought it was going to hit the floor and keep going.

'Yes, someone called Fay,'

It was the talk of the city; everyone knew about it and everyone knew that her body had not been found.

As we moved through, Phil looked at the two detectives, eyeing them suspiciously.

'What do they want with you, then?' said Phil, still giving Jason and Bruce an appraising look. Not the kind of look you want to be on the receiving end of, to be honest.

'Well,' I said, 'they want to interview me.'

The two coppers stood there, hands in pockets, itching to move through to the back office and begin their interrogation – sorry, interview.

'Just a minute,' said Phil, holding up a hand. 'Stop.' He was addressing the policemen now. 'What are you interviewing her for?'

'Well, she's given some information we need to ask her about. It's nothing to worry about, sir.'

'I don't know if I'm happy about this.'

'I'm sure it'll be all right, Phil,' I said, 'don't worry.' The truth was I already felt indebted to him for letting me use his office and I didn't really want him worrying on my behalf as well.

He looked at me. 'OK, Sally,' he said, still looking concerned. 'If you feel at all uncomfortable you come out and get us, OK?'

'OK,' I said.

Still, I felt reassured by their concern. Felt a bit safer, I suppose.

Then felt a lot less safe as the door to the back office thunked shut behind the three of us.

And once that door closed, once Phil and Grace were safely on the other side of it, all pretence at civility or friendliness simply evaporated. Jason and Bruce's body language changed. The mood in the room subtly shifted, so that I was left in no doubt who was in charge – and that I really was under suspicion.

It was a plain office. Just a table and chairs, nothing else. I was sitting at the table, thinking back on it now, like a lamb to the slaughter. Jason stood, his hands in his pockets. Bruce sat regarding me across the table, his arms folded.

I remember looking at the window, the grille across it, and thinking, 'How appropriate, there are bars on the windows . . .'

And these two, I'm telling you . . . I'm not easily spooked. There's no point in being a psychic and being easily spooked. It's like being a doctor who can't stand the sight of blood, like being a dentist who's afraid of teeth. Yet these two detectives were trying to do their very best to scare me.

And, I have to admit, it was kind of working.

Kind of. I suppose it's because they were playing out a scene. We were all playing out a scene that I had witnessed so many times before on TV and in films. A 'good cop, bad cop' routine, something like that. I wondered who would be the good cop and who would be the bad cop.

And this is how they opened proceedings.

'We believe you have lied to us, Mrs Morgan,' said Bruce.

Fighting the urge to flee, I said, 'Lied about what?' Was that a tremble in my voice?

Yes, probably.

Did they pick up on it?

Yes, probably.

'You were lying when you said you've never been to this country before,' said Bruce.

'I haven't,' I retorted quickly. My paranoia saying, *too quickly?*

'You're lying, young lady. You've been to the capital.'

(I had to control myself at that moment. *Young lady?* I didn't know whether to be flattered or offended.)

Instead I said, 'I beg your pardon, I've never been to this country before.' I gave him the date of my arrival.

'You've been to the capital before.'

'Well, it must have been in another life. You tell me when I've been to the capital.'

'Maybe it will make it easier for you to tell us the truth if we tell you that there is only one person — *one person* — who knows details about this disappearance, and he is a journalist who lives in the capital, and we believe you've visited him.'

He thumped the flat of his hand on the table.

I could feel myself filling up. Shaking my head. Trying to stop myself from crying, looking helplessly from one to the other. The one sitting on the desk had said nothing.

'Look, I'm really confused here,' I said, then, 'You do know what I do? You know my work is?'

'Well, yes, we're coming to that,' he said and he produced a little pocket diary.

It was the one I had used the night before to illustrate the image I had been given.

'Oh,' I said, recognizing it immediately, 'that's where I drew . . .'

'Yes,' he said and now he was pointing to the drawing – my drawing. 'What can you tell us about this?'

I said, 'Well, wait just a minute, I'm feeling very intimidated here and actually I think I'm going to leave the office if you don't . . .'

I made as if to stand. Now, the good cop/bad cop routine finally revealed itself. Jason was to be the good cop. He moved forward, perching himself on the side of the desk.

'Sally,' he said, 'we want you to help us if you can.'

He smiled, holding my gaze a moment, relaxing me slightly.

'Well, that's better,' I said. 'But I can't help you if you're going to keep on insisting I've been somewhere I haven't. I don't know any journalist, and if this journalist knows what I know then that's a sheer fluke, I don't know how that is. All I can tell you is that I saw a place. I saw it through the eyes of a girl and I know – somehow I just know – that girl was murdered. I later found out about Fay Raeburn disappearing. Come on, you must know I've only been in the country a short time. You must be able to check whether or not I've been anywhere else. It's not the kind of thing somebody can easily lie about. Why would I be lying to you about it anyway? You're trying to frighten me – I know you're trying to frighten me.'

'No, Sally,' said Jason, 'we're not trying to frighten you.'

Hmm, I thought. *Right.*

Still, something in the room changed at that moment. It was as though we reached an understanding and they became suddenly less intimidating. I think they began to realize that I wasn't lying – that I couldn't possibly have been lying. Which put them in a weird position, I suppose. I mean, if you're a policeman, and you're interviewing a woman from London, who simply cannot be involved in the way that you think she is, yet on the other hand you do not believe in what she does, you don't believe in psychics – well, that must put you in a strange position.

At one point, Bruce said to me, 'You know, Mrs Morgan, the information you have got . . . if you're telling us you don't know this journalist, then that means you know who the killer was.'

I shot up in my seat, suddenly petrified. Or rather, even *more* petrified. Was he really saying that I was somehow linked to the killer?

Next thing I knew, though, him saying that seemed to have opened me a little bit more, and suddenly I had a piece of information about the man responsible, which I found myself blurting out, saying, 'Well, that's a bit difficult, seeing as I've never been here before and the killer lives in this country and has never left it.'

'Does he really?' said Bruce. 'What else can you tell us about the killer, then?'

More pictures bubbled and fizzed in my mind. I saw a house. I had the impression of his ...

'*Mother*,' I said. 'I can tell you that he lives with his mother. I know that he murdered a dog when he was little. I can see his house and I can see an old car with no wheels in the front garden.'

They looked at one another.

'Go on,' said Jason. 'Tell us anything you can.'

'I see her coming out of a nightclub,' I told them.

I told them how I could see her leaving the nightclub very, very late at night. Taking a route that led her down a slight hill.

(This, it would turn out, they knew because they had footage of Fay doing this on CCTV. What perturbed them, obviously, was how I knew this, having never seen the CCTV.)

Now, though, Bruce pulled back in his seat, giving me a slightly sneering look. 'Well, that's wrong,' he said, lip curling, 'because she was never in a nightclub.'

The vision I had definitely showed her coming out of a nightclub. There was no doubt about it.

'Well,' I said, 'I'm afraid you'll just have to go back to the drawing board then, because I'm telling you that this girl was in a nightclub. She came out of that nightclub and there was a man ... yes, that's right. She was a little bit tipsy. There was a man there and he was telling her he was a cab driver.'

Another sneer from Bruce. 'That's wrong. You've got that wrong.'

146

I was so definite about this. So convinced. Remember, I was telling the police what I had seen. I had no reason to lie to them, nor was I likely to make things up just to fit. I had absolutely nothing to gain (in fact, when you think about it, I had lots to lose, the way they were treating me) from making things up about this murder. So I told them as much.

I said, 'Well, I'm sorry, then. Obviously we're not looking at the same thing, because what I'm getting is a girl leaving a nightclub, late at night, drunk, talking to a man who's telling her he is a cab driver. If that doesn't tally with your story, then it's obvious I'm seeing something completely different.'

I made as if to stand up. 'You know, I can get things wrong. Messages from the spirit world can be garbled and indistinct. It's really not an exact science, you know. No matter how much we'd like it to be.'

We'd been going round and round in circles for about half an hour, me simply telling them what I had seen and them telling me everything I had seen was wrong. It seemed that we had reached an impasse. Now, though, Bruce and Jason shared a meaningful look.

And something about their whole demeanour altered.

'Go on, then,' said Bruce, looking away.

'I beg your pardon?' I said.

'He means please tell us more,' said Jason.

'What's the point?' I said, exasperated. 'It's all wrong, remember?'

'Oh, OK,' admitted Jason, 'she might have been coming out of a nightclub.'

Still, at least they had started treating me with a little

less suspicion. I didn't feel quite so much of a prisoner any more. No longer was I worrying whether they were going to throw me in some cold, dank jail cell somewhere and leave me there to rot. That didn't mean I had started to trust them though, and for the rest of the interview me and the two detectives warily circled one another, until there came a knock on the door, and it was Phil, poking his head in the office and telling the detectives that their time was up.

They'd had about two hours with me by now and I was exhausted, saying, 'Look, we're going to have to talk about this later.'

'OK,' said Bruce. He and Jason stood, said a very curt farewell and left.

After they had gone, Phil and Grace filled me in on the details of Fay's disappearance and the two murders. Apparently, police had a suspect but they didn't have quite enough evidence to convict him. The rest of the day I carried about my business, not much the wiser, until there came another phone call: the police wanted to see me again.

Twenty-four

Unfinished business

Bruce and Jason picked me up the next morning, John giving them daggers at the door. We drove, and after a while I realized we were on a street that I felt I recognized from my vision. On the street was a building. Bruce indicated it as we approached.

'Look to your right, Mrs Morgan. Over there, that's a nightclub.'

It was a huge building and, sure enough, part of it seemed devoted to a nightclub.

'Look at the side of it,' I said, pointing. There was a little alleyway just at the side of the building, about big enough for two cars to get down. 'They went down there, and that's where his car was parked.'

'We know,' said Jason. 'And that's where we think she got in the car.'

We stood outside, me in between Jason and Bruce, who stood with their hands thrust into their pockets. They were still very sceptical, I could tell, but if past experience is anything to go by, they would be thinking, 'There's *something* here. We don't know what it is, but she's got something.'

I began recounting the details of my vision.

'She came out of there,' I said, indicating where I

meant. I pointed towards the road. 'There was a man, the man I'm talking about. He was there. He said, "Do you want a cab?" And she said, "All right." That's it. She didn't really want to at first but she agreed in the end. They walked around here ...'

Now I began trotting off to the side of the building, with Jason and Bruce hurrying behind me.

'Here,' I said, indicating where, that night, the car had been parked. 'They walked around here and when she put her head in the car, like this ...' I leant down to act it out for them. 'You know, she was just about to get into the car and he hit her on the back of the head with something.'

'What?' said Jason.

'I'm not sure,' I said, 'I can't see. But he hit her on the back of the head with something so that she fell into the car. If you ever get the car it'll have blood all over it. He's very careless. He hasn't cleaned it at all.'

'What happened next?' asked Bruce.

I looked at them both. 'Well, then he drove away. He took her to the hut.'

And that was the end of it, that day.

They returned me to the office and I continued seeing clients. It must have been a couple of days afterwards when they got in touch again. It was Jason on the phone.

'Mrs Morgan?'

Oh God, I thought.

'Yes,' I said.

'We think we may have found somewhere that fits in with the drawing you did,' he said. 'It's just around the corner from the nightclub.'

I caught my breath. Remember me saying how validation seems to open the doors of my ability? Well, it was like that. When Jason told me that they had found the hut, when he told me that the hut was near the nightclub – well, it was like one of those doors opened and I immediately knew: *this was it*. I knew it was the right place.

Sure enough, not long after I found myself in the police car again. This time, however, I was in the back seat by myself. Apparently, they now trusted me enough. For almost the first time since I met the two of them I began to relax.

That didn't last long, though. As we drove, I began to get a feeling of terrible foreboding. This was going to be the place, I thought. This would definitely be it.

Then I was thinking, *Oh my God, this place is going to be on the left-hand side*, and sure enough, there it was: an old corrugated shed as I had described it, set back on a piece of wasteland, on the left-hand side.

They stopped the car. Jason half turned in his seat to talk to me in the back.

'This piece of wasteland is about to be made into a car park,' he said. I caught my breath. Just as I had said that first night.

We got out of the car and walked on to the wasteland, which was covered with undergrowth and dry brush. We walked towards the hut.

'He brought her here,' I told them.

The two policemen – sceptical as ever – stood with their hands in their pockets, giving little away but encouraging me to tell them everything that I picked up.

'He brought her here. He took her into this place. He hung her up on a hook. He did sexual things to her.'

I looked at them, pointing behind me at the hut.

'In there,' I insisted. 'This is what I've seen. Call the forensics teams now.'

'No,' said Jason, 'they've already been.'

'And they didn't find anything?'

'No.'

'He definitely took her there. I'd lay my life on it, that he took her into that place. I think it's even the place he may have killed her. I mean, he hit her so hard on the head that she probably wouldn't have known anything about it.'

And this is where it began to unravel for me. The hut was locked so we couldn't go in. And though I insisted that the murder had strong links with the piece of wasteland – with the hut and even with a manhole cover in the area – we left with me feeling very dissatisfied, as though I hadn't been given answers, nor was I able to give them in return.

We left, I was dropped at home and I waited. By then, of course, I was keen to help the police, but the next time I heard from them was on the eve of my return to the UK. Jason called me to say, 'I'll be in London in a fortnight, I'd really like to meet up.'

'Sure,' I said.

But we didn't, and he never got in touch. I rang their office, to see what had happened, only to be told, 'The guv'nor's said we can't talk to you.'

And that was it.

I felt then – and I still feel – that Fay was killed and her body put down a well or down a manhole. 'Underground' as I said, but I had the strongest sense that it was not beneath earth. I also feel that she was taken to that hut at some point.

I feel that some really, really unpleasant things took place there.

In the end, one of the most traumatic things about that case was the fact that there was no completion or closure to it. Fay's body has never been found, and as far as I know the killer never brought to book. I had spent four days in total with the police, only for it all to come to nothing.

There was one good thing, I suppose. At least I had a very powerful sense that Fay had not suffered.

I often get this feeling with murder – that people are dead before they know about the bad things that have happened to them. I suppose this is because their killers find it easier to do what they need to do when the victim is dead. But also because killing somebody is all about exercising power over that person and power is only truly total when they are able to exercise absolute control over the body.

Don't ask me how I know this sort of stuff, I'm afraid I just do. It goes with the territory. I suppose it's because I have seen the relatives of many murder victims over the years. Then, of course, there are those murders I'm not supposed to see, but do. It's not exactly a weekly occurrence – thankfully – but probably five times throughout my career I have had a lady in my office and I've seen a murder in her background.

One time I remember very well was a woman who came to me and I told her, 'I can see a man close to you. I'm getting a yard and it has cobbled stones.'

Once again I found myself drawing a picture, a quick sketch of this yard I had in my head, the light catching the cobbles. In the yard were two men. One of them was holding a gun, which he had pressed to another man's head.

I described the man with the gun. 'Do you know this man?' I asked her.

She nodded.

'It's your husband, isn't it?'

The next day, the husband came to see me. He wanted to know what I knew.

I told him, 'You know, at the end of the day, I'm a medium – who's going to believe me?'

Which was the end of it, thankfully. Certainly it got me off the hook. But it also illustrated the problem with mediums helping in police investigations – why we are not called upon as often as we could be. It's because of the massive amount of scepticism over what we do. There is simply a level of disbelief that we have to overcome every time we so much as open our mouths. I like to believe that I helped a little in the investigation into the disappearance of Fay Raeburn, but I have no idea, because after those few days I spent helping the police, all lines of communication shut down.

I think, had they given me more time, or if we could have liaised a bit more, I could have picked up more for them, but I guess we'll never know.

*

On the whole, I prefer to work with people I can help here on earth plane. I talk a lot about wanting closure in my work, so I see myself as much more of a counsellor than I ever would an amateur sleuth, I really do. Plus I cannot change the fact that these girls are dead, which affects me so much because I have daughters of my own. I mean, I have to be quite tough to do what I do, because there's a certain amount of grief and sadness that is intrinsic in talking to dead people. But I'm not a hard cow. While I'm talking to spirits I have a kind of high that makes me want to see more and more, so the information just flows, but there is a comedown from that, too. Not a very pleasant one. And I'm not sure I can handle that comedown if I'm not actually helping to enhance anybody's life – if I'm just banging my head against a brick wall.

So I think, at the end of the day, I'd rather help those who are left behind on earth plane. Though that's not to say I shy away from dealing with murder. Oh no – in fact it is one of the main areas of my work. As you'll see.

Twenty-five

Closure for those left behind

Ever since the telly programme, and then the tour, things have been a bit manic for me. As a result, I've done far fewer one-on-one consultations. When she can though, my daughter, Fern, will schedule one in, especially if she feels it is a particularly deserving case.

This was one such case. It was the brutal killing of a beautiful young girl and the family – let's call them the Smiths – were very keen to make contact with her in the afterlife, for all the usual reasons, really: there were things about the murder in itself they had hoped to be able to resolve; plus there was some missing property they wanted to recover; and, of course, they simply wished to talk to their little girl.

At first, I was slightly reluctant to talk to them – it was such a terrible, tragic and heartbreaking crime and I wasn't sure whether or not I would be able to help. Just to digress for a moment – if somebody comes to me, there is absolutely no guarantee I will be able to reach the spirits they want to speak with; it's not like I can just pick up the psychic phone and dial a number. So in a case such as this one, where the family have such an incredible emotional investment, it would be wrong of me to agree to meet if I didn't think I could help. It would be raising their hopes unnecessarily, only to have them dashed.

In the end what I said was that I would speak to Mrs Smith, just to get a feel for her and for the case. I did that and she sounded so nice on the phone – plus I began picking things up immediately on the line – that I agreed to see them and, just before Christmas last year, they came.

As you probably know, I usually see people in my office. I decided not to in this case for two reasons. Firstly, because it was in a right state to tell the truth, full to the brim with all the stuff we take on tour; secondly, because I usually only see people one-on-one, and there were three of the Smiths: Mum, Dad and a sister. We'll call the victim Sarah.

They sat in my front room. I put them on the sofa so that I could face them and look at all three of them, all of them sitting very upright, tense, their body language betraying the fact that they were very, very nervous. The murder may have happened some years ago, but to look at the faces of this poor family you would have thought it had happened last week. This was a crime that had hit them so hard in every conceivable way. It had ravaged them, torn them apart.

Sarah had appeared to me before the Smith family even arrived. I had begun to sense her about an hour earlier, and I could feel in her a great need to speak to her mum and dad. Looking at the family, though, I knew I couldn't come right out and tell them I had Sarah here with me in the room. Somebody in my position needs to be very, very careful in a situation like that. Had I simply blurted out, 'I have a girl here with me ...' going on to describe Sarah, it would have had one of two possible effects: either they would have thought I was a complete fraud and had simply Googled an image of Sarah prior to their arrival, or it would have totally blown their minds.

Instead, I used a different tactic. I began with conversation, relaxing them, allowing them to settle. We drank some tea, we chatted about their journey, what the traffic was like, how far they'd come, what the weather was like, and so on, and so on. Gradually, they started to appear more at ease.

When I thought they were a little more relaxed, I leant forward, placed my teacup on the coffee table – it rattled slightly – then leant back to address them all.

They tensed slightly, sensing that the chit-chat was at an end.

'Right,' I said, 'do you know what I do?'

They did, of course. But, again, this is something I do to help put clients at ease and it was never more important than with this particular family. So for about ten minutes I explained to them exactly what was about to take place, further putting them at ease.

'There is one very important difference, though, with this particular case,' I said, 'and that is the fact that it is so high profile. Now, this happened a long time ago, and I won't lie to you, I read about it in the newspapers at the time. But it is not a case I took a special interest in, nor have I reacquainted myself with any of the details since. So although I know that Sarah was murdered, and I vaguely remember some of the circumstances of the case, I don't recall exact details. I just want you to know that. I don't want you thinking I am simply regurgitating something I have just read from the Internet.'

I felt it necessary to say this as, although I deal with many murders, very few of them are ever as front-page news as this one was. Often, when people come who have had a relative murdered, they want to know what really happened. In some instances, they want to know who the killer was. Well, all of this information was already available to me.

'Now,' I said, 'as I have been talking, Sarah has appeared to me. She's standing over there.'

I indicated a corner of the room, where Sarah stood, smiling at her family. Her spirit had taken on the human form for me, so it was recognizably Sarah, the Sarah that I knew from pictures I had seen in the newspaper.

Into my head came her thoughts.

Like all spirits, she began with validation and she started by telling me some details about the murder that I relayed to her family.

They were very shocking, gruesome details and I cannot repeat them here – I wouldn't want to anyway, they're far too upsetting and personal – but she gave them to me so that her family would know I was talking to her.

Like I say, this happens a lot. Spirits will give me details of the death for confirmation purposes, even though for them the actual circumstances of their death are less important in spirit world than they are on earth plane.

It is difficult for me to have to discuss such intimate and personal things with mums and dads that way. I mean, this was stuff you simply do not want to hear about your child; presumably having to hear it from the police destroyed them. Having to hear it from me, well, I cannot imagine how it must feel. I hope I never find out.

'She's sitting next to you,' I said to the mother. 'She's stroking your hand. She seems concerned about your hand. Why is your hand an area of concern to her?'

The mother smiled. Tears twinkled in her eyes. 'It's because ... because this morning I hurt it,' she said. 'Sarah must know that I hurt my hand.'

By now I knew that the family were happy that Sarah was there in the room with them. They had all the evidence they needed.

'Can you ask her ...' said the father, 'can you ask her about what was missing?'

'You've got a lot of her stuff back,' I said. They nodded. 'But she tells me that there is still one item missing.'

'What is it?' asked the father. He knew what it was – he just wanted me to say.

I told them. A lot of the material had been recovered, I said, but there was still some jewellery that had not been accounted for – that had been taken from the murder scene and never found. One of the main reasons the family wanted to speak to me in order to contact Sarah was to locate it.

I was able to tell them where I thought it was hidden. However, talking it through, we all felt that it had been removed by the killer, and that the place I saw – underneath a floorboard in a cupboard – was probably personal to him.

Sarah also had some things to say about her killer. She knew something about her killer in jail that gave her family a little comfort – something about his fate in jail.

'It saves me a job,' said Sarah's father, and I'm not sure if that was what Sarah wanted to hear on the other side, but certainly it seemed to bring her father some satisfaction. Perhaps that's why she passed on the message. Certainly what was completely absent as she spoke, was any note of bitterness or vindictiveness.

She also had some words for a neighbour of the family, who had been feeling guilty because he felt he could have done more on the night of Sarah's death, and I know that the family took those away to relay to him. She also spoke about some siblings – and this was another moment in which I confirmed to the Smiths that I definitely had Sarah in spirit, because I was given the names of the siblings, which I relayed to them, names I could not have known beforehand.

Sarah also revealed to me some of the cosmetic things done to her body to hide wounds from the attack. She was a beautiful girl, Sarah was, really interested in fashion and make-up, so this was of great interest to her, funnily enough. Again, though, it was something I could not have known and, even if I had Googled it, could not have found out from the Internet.

'She asks me to tell you not to think about him any more,' I said to her mum and dad. 'Her words are, "Don't waste any more energy on him."'

I could see the family taking great comfort from everything she had to tell them and what came through strongly during the time we spent together was that Sarah wanted her mum and dad and sister to release some of the anger and bitterness they felt in the wake of what was such a terrible crime. Sarah, in the afterlife, was happy and content. She laughed and joked with me and with her family; she did all she could to put their minds at rest.

One lovely moment came when she was talking about a baby that had been born in another part of the family, and they were all laughing about that together. She also talked about another baby expected in different part of the family, and they were all amazed; they had only heard about it themselves three days prior to the visit. Yet again, Sarah – by giving them such personal, relevant information – was just letting them know, 'I'm here. I'm on the other side but I'm OK, and I'm watching over you all.'

They missed her, they told her so, and each one of them was in floods of tears. They told me later that they had never had the opportunity to say goodbye to Sarah, and that by coming to see me they had finally had that chance.

It was an incredibly emotional meeting and a reading I will not forget in a hurry. When we had finished they went away happy, I felt, and satisfied that Sarah was in a state of contentment.

Did they fully believe, though? Does anybody fully believe? This is a question I often ask myself. And I think the answer to it must be that there is always an element of doubt.

Twenty-six

A murder and closure

Cases in which the spirit is that of somebody who has been murdered can make for some of the most emotional and traumatic readings. Let me tell you about another occasion, where a woman and her niece came to see me. I don't think I'll ever forget it, as long as I live.

As it turned out, the woman's son had been found dead in a wood. He'd been stabbed and beaten – it was horrific, I can't tell you, it really was – but his killers had never been found; all police had to go on was that they thought the poor boy had been killed by more than one person.

I discovered afterwards that it was the third or fourth anniversary of his death. It often happens that relatives of murder victims come to see me on the anniversary of the death; especially those that are unsolved. I think that members of the family hope to get some sort of closure at some point, and the anniversary of the death is just one of those times when the thought of the murder is uppermost in their mind.

In this particular case there was a certain bit of closure the mother was after. I sensed there was something she had decided she needed to know.

First, though, I needed to get her son in spirit.

Believe it or not, there are many, many murders that never make the national newspapers. Unfortunately, murder is so commonplace these days that it's not always headline news. This was one of those murders, I'm very sorry to say. It hadn't made national headlines the way that the death of Sarah had. What I'm saying is, I had absolutely no prior knowledge of the killing before the two women came to see me. Neither did they give anything away.

This happens a lot. When people come to see me they very, very rarely volunteer information about themselves. Cynics and sceptics will tell you that the way we psychics operate is to somehow elicit information from our clients. We do this, apparently, by being oh-so very clever, listening to what clients say, then using a technique called cold reading.

Cynics and sceptics don't visit psychics, though. They don't see psychics in action. If they did, they would know what I'm going to tell you now. And that is, that clients don't say a blooming thing. They've paid their money, and they want to see what you can do. And they're not stupid either. Cynics and sceptics like to believe that our clients are a rather stupid, credulous lot who will believe anything. But nothing could be further from the truth. Clients know all about hot reading and cold reading; they are fully aware of the theory that we psychics somehow wheedle personal information out of them. As a result, they sit there and say nothing.

These two ladies were no different. So, when they arrived, I had no idea at all that they were talking about murder. Instead, they sat in my office – this was a long time ago, when I was still doing one-to-one readings on a regular basis – and did what most of my clients, certainly the first-time clients do, which was to clam up completely.

However, it soon became clear. Horribly, tragically clear.

The older lady clasped her niece's hand. Tight, I could see. She asked me if I was able to contact her son.

I began to pick things up.

I had the sensation of speed. Of running feet and heavy breathing. I heard twigs snapping. Loud cracks as branches broke. I could see figures moving through the greenery and had a strong sense of conflict.

'OK,' I said, picking my words carefully. 'I've got your son here and he's ... running like mad. Did he have a hobby? Did he do paintballing or something?'

She shook her head.

'OK, I said again, treading very carefully, not sure what I was seeing and not wanting to misinterpret it.

Now I saw a man hiding.

'I can see trees,' I said. Still I had figures running through undergrowth. Still the heavy footfalls and breathing. I could hear the shake and rustle of trees and undergrowth. I heard voices, cursing, shouting. So much activity, chasing going on. None of it really made sense to me, but dutifully I relayed what I was seeing to the mother.

When I did, she screamed.

For a moment or so I thought she wasn't going to be able to compose herself. I looked at her niece, sitting beside her, holding her hand, offering her comfort.

'What's wrong, love?' I said, this image playing in my head like a film on a loop.

I still thought it was some kind of sport or something. Given the mother's reaction, though, I now began to wonder if the boy had been in the army. Perhaps I was seeing him on some kind of army exercise. Had he been killed in an accident? I didn't know. I looked at the niece for explanation. Beside her the mother had dissolved into sobs.

'What is it, love?' I pressed, leaning forward to touch the niece on her knee.

'It's Mike,' she said, 'he was murdered.'

'Oh my God,' I said. 'I'm so sorry.'

In the image there were trees, shouting, and now I began to wonder . . .

'Did it happen in a wood?' I asked.

'Yes, it happened in the trees,' she said. 'It was in, like, a spinney.'

So much of what I do is about validation. When I'm doing a reading for somebody, whether it be at home or on tour, it's all about creating a connection between me and the person I'm reading for. The spirit uses me as a conduit between them and earth plane. It is as though whenever the person on earth plane provides validation, it gives the spirit some kind of 'permission' to continue. I hope that makes sense. It's a bit like peeling the layers away from an onion. No, more like opening a series of doors. When the first door is open, you can then proceed to the next one. And so on and so on. Validation is the key I need.

However, you cannot proceed to the next door until

the first one is open. Therefore, I need a validation – I need that key – before I can proceed to the next door. When I do I then find myself receiving more information. In this case, I suddenly got much more of the picture; I had Mike, in spirit, in my head.

'They were waiting for me,' he said to me.

Now I saw men, about four or five of them, and they were chasing Mike through trees. I got a road. Yes, I saw a road.

Mike had got out of a car.

Now it came to me. Like when you're making a jigsaw and suddenly all the pieces start falling into place.

I saw the road. I saw Mike getting out of the car. I knew that he had willingly got into the car in the first place, but the men he had joined in the car wished him harm and he had realized this too late. I don't know whether he had fallen in with a bad lot or not, but that was certainly the impression that I had.

As I described the scene to the mother and her niece, the mother buried her head in her hands. I stopped, looking at the niece, wondering if I should continue. She held my gaze. She nodded.

Now, I told them, I could see Mike, running through the trees. Yes, it was like a copse, a small patch of trees, and on the other side of it was a council estate. Did he live in the council estate? No, no, he didn't live there but he knew the estate well and that was where he was heading, hoping to find some sort of sanctuary – hoping to escape from the men.

I talked them through it, all the time looking at the niece, wondering whether she would prefer me to stop.

'No,' she said, 'no, please continue, Sally. We need to hear this. This is what we came to hear.'

The men caught Mike.

They began to beat him.

One of them produced a knife.

I found out later that the mother had not been allowed to see her son because his wounds were so horrifying. All she was told was that he had died of multiple stab wounds and internal injuries, and the police thought that these had been inflicted by a group of men – that Mike had been kicked and stabbed to death.

They all had their turn, the men did. It was horrifying, truly horrifying. I spared the mother and her niece the worst of it, simply telling them that the men had beaten up Mike and he had died there, just short of the council estate.

Next, the mother and her niece wanted to know who the killers were. This was why they had come. Many of the details I'd given them – all those horrible, gruesome details of the murder – really, that was just for validation. They already knew where Mike had been killed and that there were multiple killers. They already knew about the wounds inflicted. All that did was prove I genuinely had Mike in spirit. What they really wanted to know was who did it. That was what the mother had decided she needed to know, after all this time.

And I did know. I had names. Two of them. The question was, did I give them to her?

And now came one of those instances where I'd very much have to put my trust in spirit world. I cannot say this enough, how the bond between myself and those on the other side is one of complete trust. They must truly believe in me, and in return I must trust in what they tell me. Without that trust, we have nothing together, for I couldn't possibly sit before bereaved relatives and pass on messages if I were not one hundred per cent convinced that they were trustworthy.

So, when Mike gave me two names of those involved in his death there came with it a dilemma, but for me a minor one. Yes, on the one hand you could argue that by passing on the names I was opening a potentially dangerous can of worms. After all, who's to say that the mother, once armed with those names, wouldn't have gone off and plotted revenge on those men and in doing so destroyed more lives, created more misery, endangered herself and her loved ones?

It is, of course, a very real possibility. And one that gave me pause for thought.

However, I passed on the names. Why? The simple answer is because Mike gave them to me and I truly believe that he wouldn't have done so if he knew, or even thought, it was a possibility that she might use those names to some kind of devastating end.

He knew, Mike did. Somehow, he knew that it was in his mother's best interest to have some kind of closure regarding the identities of his killers.

One of the names was quite common – it could have been anyone, quite frankly. As I said it, though, the mother and her niece were nodding as if they knew exactly who I was talking about. The other name, though, was not a name I had ever heard before. It is not a name I would have come up with in a thousand years. Yet again, the mother and the niece were nodding, saying, 'Yes, yes.'

I watched them carefully, looking at them for any sign of anger or hatred, hoping against hope that the spirit world had guided me in the best way.

What I saw in their faces, though, was not the rush to judge and to hate, but a kind of relief. As though it was a confirmation of something they already knew, and that confirmation brought them some solace. Perhaps the truth was not as bad as they had imagined. Who's to say? I was never given any details about the motives behind the killing. My own theory is that Mike had, sadly, become involved with some unsavoury elements, and that his killing had been a gang-related thing. The mother and her niece obviously knew that Mike had been involved with this world and just needed that final confirmation.

Would she do anything? I wondered, looking at her

'No,' I was told. 'No, she won't do anything.'

She was more interested in closing the lid on it, I believe. After all these years, she just wanted to know.

Sometimes, I think, it helps to know what *really* happened in any instance, because knowledge is a very, very powerful thing. It helps you overcome so many of your vulnerabilities, not the least of them fear.

Take me, for example. I have no fear of death because I understand so much of what takes place afterwards. My knowledge and belief gives me guidance, comfort and hope. I hope it will do the same for you. It's the same in a situation such as that young man's murder. The mother was empowered by knowing what had happened to Mike, and who was responsible. Prior to that, what she felt was helplessness. The mind plays extraordinary tricks, doesn't it? You can imagine something ten times worse than the truth. In this case, the truth was horrific to begin with, so I can't even imagine what Mike's mother must have been thinking. What I do know, however, is that the truth laid her mind to rest.

Now, though, she looked at me.

This was a woman who had just heard how her son was chased and beaten to death near a council estate. She had been given the names of those responsible. Yet she looked at me with great calm and great composure.

What a brave, brave woman, I thought.

'Sally,' she said, her voice small.

'Yes, darling?' I said. Me, I was still recovering myself. Back in those days I did several readings a day – at least four. There was no such thing, really, as a typical reading but, I have to say, rarely did they involve something quite as emotionally intense as that which I had just been put through. I always took a few minutes to recover after each reading, even if it had just been to help some lady talk about whether or not she should dump her boyfriend.

However, after this reading, I knew I would need a lot longer to recover. I have a strong stomach and an iron constitution – it takes an awful lot to faze me. But to see somebody chased and beaten and knifed … it took it out of me.

'When he died,' she asked, 'did he feel pain?'

I very, very rarely lie in order to protect the feelings of my clients. Sometimes I will not reveal the full extent of the truth, but if I am asked a direct question then, ninety-nine times out of a hundred, I will give a truthful answer.

I'm happy to say that I was able to do that in this instance and for the answer not to cause the mother extra grief.

'No, no, darling, he felt no pain.'

The niece looked at me sharply, as though she thought I was lying. Don't take us for fools, the look said, and I turned to her: 'No, really, in a situation such as that his adrenaline would have been so charged up he would have felt nothing. I know this. You know why? I've dealt with many, many murders in the past. Many spirits have spoken to me on this subject and they all say the same thing: I felt no pain. I promise you, darling. Every relative is like you, wanting to know. I have people who cry themselves to sleep every night thinking of the agonies suffered by their loved one in their last moments, but it just isn't like that. The body's defences kick in. Then, after that, the soul leaves the damaged body and travels to the other side. Really, pain just does not come into it.'

This seemed to satisfy them; they seemed happy about that. At least, they asked me no more questions about it. And shortly after that the reading was concluded.

I'm glad to say that it was the absolute truth about whether or not Mike felt pain in his last moments. And to be honest it would have been a similar answer in most instances. There was a time, however, that I won't forget in a hurry, when I saw great, great pain at the point of death. It was an evening event I did at a place on the outskirts of London, a health club, and there was a woman in the audience who had been married and I began picking up things about her husband — the most horrific things. She was a Middle Eastern woman. And I began to pick up the fact that her husband had been in prison in a cell.

And tortured.

I cannot begin to tell you how horrifying this image was. I've been doing this all of my life and, in all those years, this was the only time I have ever seen something to make me think, 'Please let him die, please let him die.'

Of all the violent deaths I've seen, this is the one that truly sticks in my mind, because he was being slowly tortured to death in that prison. They used electric shock treatment on his genital areas; they smashed the soles of his feet and worse.

I had never encountered anything like this before. Believe you me, I am no fan of gory films or books, therefore had no knowledge of torture techniques. It's only really in recent years that these things have become public knowledge anyway. But there it was, playing out in my head, like some kind of horrible snuff film.

Through me he told her, 'I'm happy now. Please remember, that I'm happy now.'

But, oh, how he died.

There I am telling that mother and her niece in my office about adrenaline stopping the body from feeling great pain, but this man — he died in absolute agony.

I kept this from the lady in the audience. All I told her was that her husband was in a better place now and he was happy. She had never got his body back, so I suppose at least he was able to offer her that little comfort from the afterlife.

All of those readings had a similar effect. The bereaved person comes to me hoping to find a little closure from the afterlife and the spirit world always delivers. They always go away from my office or an event feeling happier about the ultimate fate of their loved ones.

Twenty-seven

The messages we get

A liar can be a liar in spirit, a muddle-headed person can be muddle-headed in the afterlife. And so on and so on. That's the only explanation I have for the fact that I'm sometimes given wrong information. Sometimes I'll be reading for someone and nothing seems to go right and the client will say, 'It's no use, Sally. I can tell you're being given the wrong information.'

It's probably one of the most frustrating aspects of my job: why is it that I can get fifty things right and then, suddenly, for no apparent reason, I get a curve ball? Something that's completely wrong? It's not even as if it's garbled; it's just plain wrong. No other way to describe it. A load of pony.

Now, if the spirit I have been dealing with has so far been truthful, why would they suddenly lie? Is it because they were a liar in life? Or is the information somehow disrupted by another spirit? Perhaps a careless one? Or one who is malicious?

The simple answer is, I just don't know. Like so many other things about spirit world, it will have to wait until I get there for me to find out.

Why are messages sometimes wrong, I'll want to know?

Also, why are they incredibly clear sometimes, other times nonsense?

I make it a policy not to try to interpret messages. In other words, I say what I'm given. Very often this results in messages that sound like gibberish or mean nothing at the time – but will do later – or could be just downright confusing. More often than not, though, it means something to the person for whom I am reading.

I say what I hear and I rely on spirits to help those on earth plain make sense of it. Most of the time it does, and the effect can knock your head off. Other times, it doesn't. That is just one of the pitfalls of talking to spirits, I suppose. I can't pick and choose how they say what they do, or the things they say.

Not long ago I did a reading for a woman who had lost her child. I'll go into child death in a bit more detail later but suffice to say that these are often the most heart-rending readings. In this particular reading, the little boy in spirit asked me to tell his mum, 'Thank you for washing my shoelaces.'

That's all it was. Just a simple thank you. But, oh my God, it broke our hearts, it really did. And you know what? I think a message like that performs two functions. Firstly, it satisfies the sitter that I really do have their child in spirit – the right little boy – because, as I've said, one of the things I always have to deal with in my job is the burden of proof; when people come to see me, or when I talk to people at shows, however much they believe in what I do, they are still looking for that extra bit of corroboration. So if I blurt out, 'Thank you for washing my shoelaces,' that is the proof they need that they are in touch with their loved one. Because how on earth could I, Sally Morgan, know that she used to wash her child's shoelaces? I mean, it's a bit random, isn't it? Speaking personally, I don't think I've ever washed a pair of shoelaces in my life, or if I have, then certainly not regularly enough to be thanked for it. Yet this particular woman, it blew her away. She knew exactly what I was talking about.

But why was this as far as the message went? Why no more than 'thank you for washing my shoelaces'? Well, I have no answer to that. Perhaps the spirit simply had nothing else to say. He wanted to thank his mother, he wanted to show her that he was still with her. Who can say? I don't translate, I don't analyse. I don't alter what the spirits tell me or try to make it 'fit'. I just have to trust them to give me the right messages.

Like the woman in Blackburn whose ex-boyfriend was a kickboxer. When I said 'spark', she nearly fainted. It took that one bit of proof for her to know that I was on the level. After all, there was no way I could have known those bits of information. In no way could I have known that her boyfriend, whose nickname was Sparkle, had told her in bed one night that he was a killer.

To many people that may have been a strange thing to say. After all, 'spark' – it could have meant anything. What I'm saying is that what seems like gibberish to one person can be extraordinarily relevant to somebody else.

Why, I am sometimes asked, do the spirits use their rare opportunity to speak to their loved ones on earth plane merely to pass on what you might think of as being fairly mundane or trivial messages?

I know what they mean, it does seem strange sometimes, the things they say. Sometimes they'll say something you can tell is really important like, 'Don't buy that motorbike.' Other times it's something that seems so small. Again, it's one of those things I just can't easily explain. After twenty years of marriage, why make some apparently innocuous comment about the back door not being locked? Why not use that one opportunity you have to make some incredibly profound declaration of love, or reveal some desperately important secret or warning?

Well, again, this is all down to interpretation, all down to the person involved. Not every message will be of paramount importance, some kind of life-saving bit of advice. As often as not it will simply be a thank you for washing shoelaces.

Imagine you're a spirit, for a moment. Let's say it's a Wednesday night, it's cold, it's been raining and the person you most love in the world has come to see a medium, hoping to get a message from you. They're sitting there feeling a bit chilly, maybe shivering slightly. What would you say?

Probably: 'God, darling, why didn't you put that overcoat on? You'd be much warmer.' Because that's how you would feel at that exact moment. Your heart would go out to your poor old hubby, cold and shivering, and you'd revert back into caring mode. I know I would anyway.

Another thing I sincerely believe about my work – and something I mention during almost every show – is that we have to trust that the messages we get are the messages we're *meant* to get.

I know that sometimes people come to the show and

are disappointed – either by the fact that they haven't got a reading or by the messages they have received. It's the same when people come to see me individually. They arrive thinking they want to hear one thing and their loved one tells them something totally different. It blows them away all right, but they think, 'Bloody hell, I never wanted to hear that.' It's not what they *wanted* to hear; it is what they were *meant* to hear.

Through a medium, however, spirits have the opportunity to deliver a very specific message: Don't let our little boy buy that red car. Make sure you wear stout shoes next Thursday. Wrap up warm next February, especially around the neck.

Not long ago, at a show, I spoke to a woman in the audience, and told her I had her husband on stage with me.

'Why does he want me to thank you for the fork and trowel?' I asked her, thoroughly confused. If ever there was a random message from a spirit, that was it.

It turned out she'd had him buried with them.

The audience burst out laughing and it was a nice, warm moment.

'What were you hoping he would do? Dig himself out?'

Now the audience was in hysterics. Again, though, we were all having a laugh together. Nobody ever gets laughed *at*, at my shows.

'You know what? For a moment I thought I was going mad,' I said. 'He was telling me to thank you for burying him with his trowel and his fork.'

They say things that are relevant to the moment, that is what I think. Cynics and sceptics say, why don't spirits warn us about the terrible things ahead? Why didn't spirits warn us about 9/11, for example? Well, for a start, they did, because I predicted that; the problem is, of course, that I am a medium and many people think mediums are completely loopy, so who's going to listen? But in the main, I feel that spirits who deliver profound messages are usually people who were like that anyway. Some spirits simply want to chat to members of their family. Some spirits feel they have to say something of great importance. In spirit, as on earth plane, we are all different. We all have differing concerns, worries, fears. We all want different things. Plus, I think that spirits are most preoccupied with protecting their loved ones rather than delivering warnings on any kind of global scale. What I encounter time and time again is people describing near-death experiences who tell me they feel they were saved by 'a thought', which somehow came from the spirit of their mother or father or grandfather. This happens all of the time. It goes back to this idea that spirits are constantly watching over us. I really believe this, I really do.

So your next question is, *If I have a spirit that looks after me, how come he let me break my leg that time on holiday?* I mean, surely it would be nice to think that your granddad might provide you with some guidance, a warning perhaps, some signposts as to what will happen to you. 'Watch yourself on the slopes today,' something like that.

And then, perhaps more importantly, what about death?

Now, I don't like to see death, I don't want to be shown it and I have made a pact with him upstairs that I won't be shown it.

Can you imagine how traumatic it would be to look around a theatre full of people who have come to see you and know that a certain percentage of them are due to die before the year was out, or within the next three years?

I couldn't do it. It would be horrible – too horrible for words. So I made this pact with him upstairs – yes, I suppose I am talking about God – I said, 'I'll do this but if anyone has to know they are going to die, then I'm afraid you are going to have to find your own way of telling them. I just don't want that kind of responsibility.'

I say this to him all of the time, just so he knows I mean it. And there's no doubt that he's listening. Or, at least, someone is listening, because in return for passing messages between this world and the afterlife I have been granted that one small favour: I don't see death.

But, if I did see death, would that mean I'd spend every reading and every show passing on messages about it? Bob, you have to stop smoking. Jane, don't get on a bus on 26 February. Fred, don't go on holiday this year.

I don't think so.

You are on a journey with a preordained destination and spirit world understands this. Those in spirit realize that nothing they can say will change that journey. If it is written in your lifespan then it is going to happen. After all, if it was you, would you want to know that some kind of horrible death was what lay in store for you? *A death you could not possibly avoid?*

I know I wouldn't.

Twenty-eight

Death on tour

During a tour, I did a show where the most incredible thing happened. Now, this was one of those exceptions to the rule, where somebody on the other side wasn't particularly happy.

I had a man on stage with me who had been killed.

'I have a man here,' I said to the audience, 'and I'll be honest with you, he's at peace but he's very angry. In fact, it's almost as if he's spitting with anger. I think his name is Don or Ron. And I think he wants two people here. Does that mean anything to anyone?'

'Up here, Sally,' came a voice.

'This is not pleasant,' I said.

And it wasn't. It was funny, but I'd had a feeling about this show since way before it had started. The last time I felt that way was before the filming of *Star Psychic* – the one with the belly dancer. This wasn't quite as forceful as that, but it was similar – a feeling of foreboding. As before, I'd had difficulty placing the feeling. Just like then, though, I suddenly knew . . .

He was a big chap, wearing a football shirt. A member of the crew gave him a microphone.

'What have you done?' I said to him, as carefully as I

could. Around us the auditorium fell quiet. Everybody held their breath.

'He came to my house, Sally.'

And never left it, I knew, feeling a chill.

'I'm really upset by this, I've got to be honest with you, darling. I've got a man here, what's his name? Don or Ron?'

'Ron.'

'Why do I feel the saliva is coming out of my mouth?'

'He attacked me in my house.'

'So was he spitting at you? Foaming at the mouth?'

I felt very strongly that this Ron – the dead man – had some kind of liquid at his mouth. What it was, I couldn't be sure. At first I thought it was saliva or foam. The man in the audience didn't confirm it.

Still, though, I could see great anger, could feel great violence.

'He attacked me,' he added. 'I was defending myself.'

I steeled myself, wondering if I should say what I wanted to ask . . .

'Did you kill him?' I said at last, again very carefully.

'My son did,' he said.

An audible gasp. A shockwave that ran through the theatre.

'Look,' I said, 'I'm not pointing the finger at anyone, because at the end of the day we have to do what we have to do at any given moment . . .'

'He came to my house with another man.'

'Wait,' I said, 'I really don't know if I'm keen on what I am seeing here with this man. This man seems as though he's out of control. Does that make sense?'

The man and his wife nodded.

'I've got to carry on with tonight. We've got all these other people here and I want this man to leave me now.'

The simple fact of the matter was that I had no clear idea of what had gone on at the house. A man had been killed, that much I knew. I had his spirit there with me on stage but I didn't know then, and still don't, what his motive was for appearing to me. I don't know why he wanted to speak to the two people in the audience. Here I am, banging on and on about how the spirit world is always motivated by love – you must be sick of hearing it by now – but I really couldn't say for sure whether or not that was the case here.

At one point the spirit said to me, 'Send my love to . . .' and he gave me a woman's name.

I relayed the name. 'Who is that?'

The man in the football shirt said, 'That's my partner,' and he indicated the woman sitting beside him. She put her hands to her face, already in tears.

'She was knocked to the ground as they burst through the door,' said the man in the football shirt.

So why was the victim sending her his love? Was it some kind of sick taunt? I had a very strong sense of being 'used' somehow.

In the end, it was a case of 'don't go there'. This was one can of worms I wanted the lid firmly closed on.

There was one thing yet nagging me, though. As I dismissed the spirit – or tried to, at least – I felt that I needed to say one last thing to the pair in the audience.

'You don't still live there, do you?'

'Yes,' said football shirt man. 'My son is doing six years for manslaughter.'

More information came to me. I was seeing a small window. This was the window in the front door, I was sure of it. The image wouldn't leave me. And I was getting this frothing, this foaming at the mouth again.

The spirit stayed on stage with me, feeding me this image.

'He was off his nut, this man,' I said, still trying to get rid of the spirit. Still having difficulty doing so.

It was as if there was a little tug of war between us. I wanted rid of him but every time I tried to eject him from the stage he gave me a little bit more information, pulling me back in.

It gets like that sometimes. I really wasn't sure about this guy, not at all.

'He was foaming at the mouth,' I said. 'And I think he still feels this way. This is not good.'

Then it came to me. This was it, this was the reason why his spirit was appearing to me. Somehow he had become trapped – or part of him, at least – and I knew . . . I had the answer.

'He comes to you,' I almost shrieked. 'Oh my God, you've got to let him go, he comes to your house. He wants to be let go. Do you have a rug in your hallway?'

They looked at me, the pair of them in the audience. I felt for them, I really did, their lives being laid bare like this. But I knew I had to do something to solve this problem.

The man raised the microphone to his mouth, his hand

shaking slightly. 'The hallway is where the fight took place,' he said.

I knew it. The information hit me like a brick. Even so, I knew it. It was the rug.

'You don't still have it, do you?' I asked, knowing what the answer would be.

He nodded.

'Well, you've got to get rid of it. You've got to get rid of it now. Put it in the bin, roll it up, put it in the bin. You need to be free of this spirit.'

He nodded. Beside him his wife nodded too.

And suddenly, the spirit on stage with me was gone. It was as though he felt 'my work here is done' and he left me in peace.

And thank God he did. That reading was one of those truly traumatic occasions I can quite frankly do without, thank you. There was a certain moral ambivalence about it that I found unsettling. Put it this way: I didn't finish the reading with any clear idea of who was right and who was wrong. I had no sense that the spirit was good or bad. All I achieved, really, was to – hopefully – sever that last, unwanted tie between them. I'm learning all the time in my work. Not all spirits are healing spirits, I have found. And this one, I wasn't so sure about.

It was quite a relief, I can tell you, to get on with the rest of the show.

Twenty-nine

Suicide and the spirit world

If murder is one of the most distressing ways to lose a loved one, then perhaps suicide is even worse.

I suppose the question those left behind must always ask themselves is: why, why, why?

Let us not get carried away though. Suicide is a form of death just like any other death, yet on the other hand it's unique in that it requires so much explanation. It always leaves people with answered questions, anger and bitterness. I get a lot of people who come to see me who need help with a suicide victim's last words, usually left in the form of a note – or not.

I'll give you an example of a woman I saw, Kate, who had issues about the death of her brother, Finn. He'd committed suicide and Kate felt that he had written a note but she'd never seen it; she'd always believed that her parents had hidden the note from her or destroyed it. The note had been bitter, she was sure of it. She thought he had been angry with their parents and would have said as much.

Now she wanted to know, had there really been a note? Was she right?

Sometimes, in a situation like that, I don't know what's for the best. That's the reason I don't interpret. It's because I trust spirit world; I have faith that those in spirit world want only the best for those on earth plane. So if a spirit passes me information that seems as though it might be damaging or emotionally loaded, I give myself no choice but to pass that information on. That's the faith I place in spirit world.

So I told Kate exactly what I was told, that, yes, Finn had written a suicide note, and that the suicide note had expressed anger towards their parents – and that the note had been destroyed.

Finn had a girlfriend. She had died some months before, when she fell from a building. At first the death was believed to be suicide, but Kate had her doubts. Not long before seeing me, Kate had attended an art exhibition to celebrate the life of the dead girl, who had been a sculptor. A brilliant artist by all accounts; Kate spoke in glowing terms of her work. However, at the exhibition the dead girl's friends had been hostile towards Kate. They blamed Finn for her death and because Finn wasn't around – he was dead – they took it out on Kate.

Once again I was able to lay her mind at rest. The dead girl hadn't deliberately killed herself; she'd fallen. Like Finn, she was happy and contented in spirit world. In spirit world Finn and the dead girl were together – together in a way that had tragically been denied to them in life.

I like to feel that Kate finished the reading that day a happier, less tormented person. It's at times like that that I want to turn to spirit world and give the big thumbs up, a round of applause. Good job, well done, guys. You came through again.

Having said all of that, my theory on notes – and I don't want to upset anyone here, so I want to tread very carefully – is that they never really tell the whole truth.

In a note, someone might say, 'I cannot live any more. I cannot live without Mary.'

To me, that's not really a reason to kill yourself, it is simply a trigger, and the actual reason for doing it – taking one's own life – is far, far more complex than that; hidden at much deeper levels, too. To kill yourself with 'I can't live without Mary' as a reason ... well, it isn't really a *reason*, I would say. In fact, I'd argue, it's blame. It's apportioning blame. No, the real reason is much too deep for those of us left on earth plane to ever make sense of.

That doesn't stop us trying, though, and of course we rely on the suicide to give us the information we need to try and make sense of the death. So, when they don't leave a note, it can cause great, great pain.

I had a case a while back where a woman came to see me. She'd come about her son, but didn't tell me at first. She sat down opposite me, giving me no information, as is usual with clients. Every reading is a test. Nevertheless, as she sat opposite me, I could see who it was she had come to contact. I had her son in spirit.

Oh, such a young one, too. Heartbreaking. He was all of fourteen years old.

The first thing I had from him was a bicycle. I could see a bicycle lying on the ground in what was obviously a wooded area. I could see a monkey bar, on which he had tried to rest his bicycle. That's what we used to call them back when I was young, monkey bars. I don't know what they call them now. But this is what I saw, a monkey bar, against which he had tried to rest his bicycle.

I told her what I could see. She looked at me blankly.

I wasn't getting it. For some reason, I wasn't getting what she had come for.

'What I am seeing is a path,' I said. 'It was a path put there years and years before.'

She nodded.

Now I began to receive more information. Do you remember what I was saying before? How, when you get a better validation, you then start to get more detail? This was one of those times.

Yes, the path was placed years and years before, and there was a hand rail put there to help people as they walked along the path.

This was what the poor young boy in spirit had tried to rest his bike against. But the bike had fallen off it. The image I had in my head was of this monkey bar – hand rail, whatever you want to call it – sticking up from a bed of leaves and undergrowth. By the side of it was this young boy's bicycle.

'I can see the bicycle,' I told her.

She sat there.

I'll tell you something else about the weird dynamic that takes place when I'm doing a reading. The person only has to move their eyes. There only needs to be a minimal movement of the face. Then I know I'm spot-on.

It was the same with this woman. There was something about the way her face moved slightly as I spoke that let me know I was on the right track.

The image seemed to expand and I began to take in more of what I was being shown.

Suddenly, I realized what had happened. The boy had ridden his bike into the woods, he had tried to lean his bike against the monkey bar, but in his haste it had simply fallen to the floor. Then – he had climbed up on to a tree, on to a branch. I saw him pull from his rucksack something that might have been a washing line or rope.

And . . . oh no.

He hung himself.

I didn't tell his mother I had seen all of this. You can't. You simply cannot splurge all of this information to a grieving relative. No way can you just say to someone, 'Oh my God, your son hung himself.' It would destroy them. You have to be gentle, and I was. Any other way would be cruel, unfair, unprofessional.

I hadn't even told her that I had her son in spirit.

For the time being, I simply said, 'I have a young boy here.'

It is very, very quiet in my office. There are times, when I have a client, that it seems almost as if we are no longer in a house on the outskirts of London, but somewhere else, as though there is no sense of time or place. There is something about the heat of grief, of love, of emotion, that will do that to a place.

It was as though we were alone in the world.

'Is it your son?' I said.

Opposite me, I saw her fold slightly; she seemed to shrink in the wake of what I had said.

'Yes,' she said.

'Oh, darling, I'm so sorry . . .' I paused. I looked at her, she returned my gaze. We both knew. 'He took his own life, didn't he?' I said.

'Yes,' she said, closing her eyes. For a moment I thought she might stay that way, in silent mourning. But then she seemed to gather some inner strength and she opened her eyes, looking at me.

'His name was Thomas,' she said.

'You don't know why he did it, do you?' I said.

She shook her head, no. Then began to speak. She told me that he was a loving boy. That he was loved in return. Oh, and you could tell that they loved him to death, his family; that he was their pride and joy. He wasn't being bullied at school – or, indeed, anywhere. He had lots of friends, he enjoyed school. This poor family simply could not understand why their little boy would kill himself.

In my head was the most upsetting, heartbreaking image. It was green, so green, trees and hedgerows and undergrowth everywhere. Thomas's bicycle lay on the floor of the wood and for all intents and purposes it was a lovely, pastoral image.

Except for this young man hanging dead from a tree.

'Why?' she asked me. 'Why did he do it?'

As she spoke I was given access to his thoughts. I could literally tell exactly what he was thinking, and it broke my heart, because at that moment I knew just why he'd done it.

It was simply an act of curiosity.

There was nothing more to it than that. Nothing more sinister. This young lad had a happy life, happier than many other children his age. You could even argue that he was a brighter, more intelligent boy than most; that he had a more enquiring mind. It was simply the case that he wanted to know what it was like to hang himself.

Perhaps he had seen it on television or in a film. I was not allowed that far into his head. All I knew was that in his head he had the question, 'What's it like?'

Just a normal kid.

A bright kid.

But we all do irrational things. I mean, have you ever looked in a fire and wondered about putting your hand into the flames? Have you ever done anything that some little instinct told you was a bit stupid, but you just wanted to know how it felt?

Chances are you did something a bit silly and it had no far-reaching consequences. Chances are you just felt a bit silly, that's all.

Not in this case.

He thought, 'I'll put this around my neck and jump off this branch.'

I said to her, 'Have you watched any films where he'd seen someone hanging from a tree?'

'No,' she said. 'I don't think so.'

I leant forward to touch her knee, saying, 'You know what? I think he must have done. I think your son saw something, whether it was on TV or on a film, or perhaps he read something, but I think that his imagination was fired by what he had seen and this was ... I hate to say it, darling, I really do. I think this was just an experiment that went wrong. What I am getting here is Thomas thinking, "I'll tie this rope on this tree and put it around my neck and jump, I bet I can get out of that." He didn't intend to kill himself, darling, he's telling me that. He didn't think that what he was doing would kill him.'

She looked at me. I wonder what she felt at that moment. I wouldn't like to hazard a guess.

'Are you saying it was an accidental death?' she asked me.

'Yes,' I said. 'It was an accidental death.'

'He wants to say something to you,' I added.

I could see a huge sob about to escape. Her fist went to her mouth.

'He wants to say to you, "I'm sorry, Mum, I didn't mean to do it. I am so sorry to have caused you all of this pain.'''

Now the sob escaped. Tears began flowing down her cheeks. I reached to the box of tissues at my side, plucked two or three out in quick succession and passed them across to her. She took them, gratefully, snuffling a thank you. In my head I heard birdsong. My heart ached for him, for childhood – a life – cut short.

For what? A whim. Curiosity. It hardly seemed fair.

'Where is he?' she managed.

'In the afterlife,' I said to her. 'He's in the afterlife. I can see him with . . . ' he was with other members of their family.

'He watches over you,' I said. 'He's there.'

What I didn't say, of course, was that it was his time. What he said to me was that he fully accepted his moment had come to pass over. Something like that, though, you don't say that to a grieving relative; it just doesn't seem right.

When she left she took with her the knowledge that

her son had been happy during his life; that there was nothing she or anyone else could have done to prevent what was, in the end, a horrible, freak accident. She also took away the knowledge that her son was happy in the afterlife. Certainly, it was a very disturbing and emotionally draining reading, but like most, it ended with comfort for the person on earth plane.

Thirty

A pink, fluffy diary

Suicide has a stigma attached to it, even in these supposedly enlightened times.

Some religions, especially Catholicism, believe that it is a sin to take your own life and that when a suicide is passed to the other side they will go to hell. Well, I don't believe any of that. I think it is all balderdash. You cannot tell me that a lot of the people I deal with in my work are bad souls who deserve to go to hell. In my experience, most suicides are young males, and they probably do what they do – I'm very sad to say – either on impulse or out of sheer, youthful stupidity. Young boys, schoolboys, take their life by hanging. In their teenage years, victims use tablets. Older men go back to hanging. That's what I have found anyway.

What I do know is, when they get to the other side they're treated exactly the same as somebody who died of natural causes.

I don't just believe this, I am certain of it. If you have a relative who took their own life, please do not worry. They are enjoying the afterlife in exactly the same way as somebody who died naturally.

Remember, to those of us left behind, suicide can sometimes seem like an 'unnatural' way to die and many of us on earth plane feel quite offended by the very idea of suicide. Why, we wonder, would somebody want to take their own life, remove themselves from this wondrous existence we call life? Some think it's a crime, even.

I actually think the worst thing somebody can do is to judge using earth-plane values. There are those who say suicide goes against everything that life is about, and is sacrilegious. Well, why? Why does it? It goes against a set of values we have agreed upon on earth plane, that's all. If life was that precious, no one would ever die, and suicide is a form of death just like any other. We all have our time – that date stamped on our forehead when we're due to leave earth plane. Suicide is just one way off it. If we don't get knocked over or die of disease, then we will take our own life. We cannot help but abide by our given date. I mean, it is more complex than that, because most people who take their own life are suffering from some form of mental illness, be that mild depression, severe depression, schizophrenia, whatever. There is a chemical imbalance in the brain, there's got to be, because it's not rational to think, 'I'm going to kill myself.'

Still, that doesn't change the fact that we have a time limit which is different for all of us and, whether we like it or not, some suicide falls into that.

Maybe if we somehow knew the date stamped on our forehead we might actually be able to work out how we were going to die. For example, if you're a truck driver and you know that you're due to die on 25 July, the day after your forty-second birthday, you might say, 'Oh God, I'll probably die in my truck.'

Who would want that, though? No thanks. What

would happen? You'd take the day off work and stay in bed and your bedroom ceiling would collapse on you.

In spirit world, when a suicide passes, spirits simply say, 'We have to go and collect that person, they've passed. He was a good man, she was a good woman. He or she just could not handle being on earth plane.'

I will never forget a woman who came to see me one day. As usual, I knew nothing about her circumstances before she arrived and neither did she tell me before the reading began. She sat, her legs jiggling nervously. Straight away I picked up a young girl, and I could see a window at the top of a building.

It was a sash window, in the old style, in an old building.

The window was open and sitting on the ledge was the girl. She sat with her feet inside the room and was talking to somebody.

I described what I could see to the woman in my office.

'Oh,' I said, 'is this your daughter?'

The lady didn't say anything. Her hands were clasped in her lap, knuckles whitening. One of those moments, as I was saying before, where it only takes the tiniest bit of body language to give me exactly the validation that I need for the reading to continue.

She pulled something out of a bag that she had with her. It was a pink, fluffy – well, at first I thought it was a purse, but then I realized it was a diary – a pink, fluffy, fur-covered diary.

'Oh my God,' I said, 'it is your daughter, isn't it?'

She nodded slowly.

'She fell out of the window?'

'Yes,' she said, 'yes.'

Fell?

Was it an accident? For a second or so I floundered, the spirits leaving me stranded momentarily as I reached for the answer. *No, she did not fall*, I realized, as the thought formed in my head that she did not fall. Yet, opposite me, her mother – still clutching the pink, fluffy diary – was nodding forcefully.

She wants to believe that I fell.

The sentence came fully formed into my head.

I did not fall. I jumped.

'Darling,' I said to the mother, 'I got it wrong. She didn't fall.'

'Oh, but you said . . .'

'Yes, I know what I said but, darling, she didn't fall, do you know that?'

She did not want to believe it, I could tell.

Now she had gone from nodding forcefully to shaking her head, just as forcefully. Looking back, I think she had come to me for confirmation of the fact that her daughter had fallen, rather than taken her own life. What I was telling her now was not what she wanted to hear.

But as I have said many times before, I do not censor the messages I'm passed from the afterlife, and the message I was being given now was most definite: *I did not fall, I jumped.*

'No,' said the mother, eyes gleaming with tears, looking nervously towards the door of my office as though she wanted to escape. 'She wouldn't have jumped. She loved her life. She loved us and we loved her. She knew that.'

Another flash of knowing came to me. Or, should I say, was given to me. 'There was someone else in that room. Wasn't there?'

She jumped slightly. I had hit a nerve.

'Well,' she said, 'I think there was someone else in the room, yes, a boy, but everyone is telling me that there wasn't.'

'Why do you think there was someone else in the room?' I asked her.

She lifted the diary for me to see. 'It's this,' she said. 'This diary was found down the corridor. My daughter never let this diary out of her sight . . .'

'She kept it on a small table near a music centre, didn't she?' I said.

Flash.

Again, an image that just came to me. A picture of the different decks of a record player.

She smiled, a sad smile of recognition and memory and longing.

'Yes, that's right, Sally,' she said, and she began to cry, very quietly.

I reached forward to touch her arm, saying gently, 'I know, I know.'

Now I could see a picture, in pin-sharp focus, of the room. Her daughter, sitting on the window ledge, her feet inside the room, window open. The music centre. Somebody else in the room, and they were talking. An animated conversation. No, it was an argument. She was arguing with a young man.

I think it was a relationship that was ending. Because now the two of them both seemed to be crying. They were arguing, quite angry with each other, but sad, too; definitely young love coming to an unhappy end.

The boy strode to the music centre and picked up her diary. You would have expected the girl to have reacted, to push herself off the window ledge and come running up to him to snatch back her diary. Part of me *needed* her to do that. I wanted her to get off the window ledge and grab the diary back and take the boy by the shoulders, push him out of the room, slam the door behind him and get on with her life.

For her mum, I wished that. But no, the boy whirled and left the room, still carrying the girl's diary. She watched him go, on her face an unreadable look. A mixture of resignation, of sadness, of something else I couldn't decipher.

The door slammed behind him and he was gone, having left the picture for good – having left her life for good.

Why he took her diary, I do not know. I had a sense that contained within it were details of the love affair. Or, rather, he *thought* that contained within it were details of the love affair; that, perhaps having flicked through it – maybe in the corridor outside – he realized his mistake and dropped it.

I guess there must have been anger and bitterness there, for him to drop the diary in the corridor, but if there was any it came from him, not from her – certainly not as far as she showed, for she remained seated on the window ledge for many moments after he was gone.

It's funny, because even though I knew the outcome – knew exactly what was about to take place – I found myself willing it not to happen. Thinking, *Please don't do it, darling, please. For your mum. For your family who all love you so much. Just don't do it.*

Funny, isn't it? Even though her date was that day and there was nothing she could do to prevent destiny taking its course, nothing I could do either, I still willed it not to be.

Then, she was gone. One moment she was there, absorbing the impact of the argument, dwelling upon it, deep in a dark, dark place in its aftermath; the next she had pushed herself backwards and out of the window.

'I regretted it as I fell,' she told me.

Oh, and my whole being ached for her.

'Will you tell her?' she said to me. 'Will you tell her that I didn't mean to hurt her; that I regretted it?'

She was at peace in spirit world and I was able to pass the sentiment on to her mum. Even so, it was one of those situations where I really needed to trust in what I was being told. The girl obviously knew that her mother would feel comforted by her words, and I could see this was the case, ultimately. For although she spent many moments crying in my office, when she did stop, there was a certain calm about her.

It's like what I was saying before about how sometimes it's the knowing that gives us comfort and reassurance. It may not be what we want to hear, but at least we know. We say 'rest in peace' when it comes to the dead. Perhaps in actual fact it's us who need to do that.

Thirty-one

I didn't see children

I have one more story about suicide to tell you. It concerns a 23-year-old boy called Graham, who was a friend of Fern, my daughter. Well, a friend of a friend really. Either way, the family connection was how he had managed to get an appointment, because otherwise I was booked solid – I am always booked up over a year ahead, believe it or not. This was when I was about to start filming *Star Psychic*, and I was just seeing the last few people before work on the series commenced.

Also, he was a soldier, who had just got back from Afghanistan, which was another reason I agreed to slot him in.

It was a lovely sunny day that day. He knocked and I opened to find this young lad wearing combat trousers and work boots, and a sleeveless white vest. He had tattoos, short hair, blond. You could tell he was in the army. He had that army look about him. He was very good-looking and was obviously very fit.

After he'd come in and we'd got settled with a bit of chit-chat, I said to him, like I say to everyone, 'Have you ever seen a medium before?'

'No,' he said, and I noticed something about him,

something about the way he sat, very upright and very intent. Yes, perhaps it was something to do with his army background, but I also put it down to nerves.

Little did I know then, but that reading would prove to be one of the biggest dilemmas of my life.

'What is it I can help you with?' I asked him, having explained what it is that I do.

He looked at me very strangely. Something about his body language wasn't quite right. I was open and I saw that with him was a much older man in spirit, who I knew to be his grandfather.

'I'd like to know, Sally . . .' he started.

After a pause, I prompted him, 'Yes, darling?'

There was another pause, then he seemed to change tack slightly, saying, 'What's all this about an afterlife then?'

Just like that. Sort of jolly and carefree.

'Well, there is an afterlife, darling,' I said.

'How do you know?' he asked me.

I've done enough readings in my time to know whether a client is seeking validation. 'Well, I'll tell you,' I said. 'Because I have your granddad here.'

He looked at me, his eyes widening somewhat, his expression urging me to continue.

'His name is Bill,' I added.

I watched him absorb this information.

He said, 'My granddad is with me?'

'Yes, he is, darling.'

He nodded, taking it in, thinking about it for a moment. He looked so young and vulnerable, I wanted to reach across and hug him.

'So, when you die then,' he said, 'what do you do? Do you go to this . . . heaven?'

'Yes,' I told him. 'Yes, you do.' And I told him about heaven and hell. How his heaven would be a kind of tailor-made heaven, designed especially for him. I told him everything that I've told you, in other words.

Again, he took it in, nodding.

Next, I began to pick up things about a relationship that had turned bad for him. The poor dear, he had really, really cared about this girl, but he'd gone into the army and she had broken things off; she just didn't want to know any more, because he was away so much.

He looked downcast at this, even as his grandfather offered words of comfort and reassurance.

'I really loved her,' he said quietly.

'I know you did, darling, I know you did,' I said.

He looked at me. 'Do you think I'll ever have kids, Sally?' he said, 'because, you know, I really love children.'

'Oh, you will make a great dad, Graham,' I said, 'but I can't see children at the moment.'

I remember thinking at the time how much I wanted to see children for him. I could sense that he would make a wonderful parent, but somehow they weren't there. I put it down to the fact that he was still such a young man. But then, as I looked harder, I came to the conclusion that he wasn't destined to have children. I didn't tell him that, though.

Since then it has become tragically apparent why I saw no children in his future.

It was because he was destined to die. His date was near.

And no, I didn't see that. For some reason, I have no idea why – one more thing to ask spirit world when I get there – this aspect of his fate was denied to me. Perhaps it is because of that deal I made with him upstairs where I asked him not to show me death. That can be the only explanation for it, really. Otherwise, I would have seen it – I'm sure I would.

Graham cried during the reading, quite a lot. There were other people in spirit who came to him. Now I look back on it, more than usual, and there was obviously a reason for that. Every mention of his granddad brought more tears.

As the reading drew to a close – or so I thought – I said to him, 'You haven't half got a big decision coming up, you know.'

'Have I?'

'Yes. I see a big decision in about seven weeks' time.'

He nodded, eyes lowered.

'Are you going to be somewhere in seven weeks?' I asked him.

He began crying again. I reached for tissues, passing them to him. 'Oh, darling, what's the matter?'

'I can't go back,' he said, his hand going to his eyes, forefinger and thumb squeezing the bridge of his nose as though to try to stem the tears.

'Can't go back to where?' I said.

'The Middle East,' he said. 'They want me to go to Iraq in seven weeks and I can't go back.'

'Oh, darling, have you spoken to your commanding officer?'

'No, it's no good. It's no good. I can't go back,' he said,

repeating himself so that for a moment or so I worried that I might lose him completely.

'Yes, you can,' I said, trying to give him strength.

'No, I can't,' he said, looking at me with red eyes.

'Graham, what's the matter?'

There was so much troubled energy around him. It was filling my room all of a sudden: impenetrable and so thick. It's difficult to describe, but it was as though he had stood, kicked back his chair and began smashing my room to pieces, only not with his fists and feet, but with a kind of psychic energy. It seemed to pulse off him. I wanted suddenly to escape from it, instead sitting right back in my chair as though feeling g-force on my chest.

'What happened, Graham?' I asked, trying to keep it together.

I will never forget what happened next. Graham's hands were at his face, as though trying to hide himself from me. He palmed away tears then placed his hands at his side, sitting up straight, composing himself. He sniffed slightly, gathering himself together, and began to speak.

'It was when I was in Afghanistan,' he said. 'I was with three other lads – there were four of us altogether – and we had to go into, like, a house. Well, you know, Sally, it's not like a house. Things are so different out there. It's like the kind of thing you see on TV, like one room, but a mud house, like a mud hut. Can you picture the kind of thing I mean?'

I nodded, not wanting to say anything, not wanting to break the spell.

He took a deep breath and continued. 'We knew that the Taliban were in there. We went in, no messing about;

we just smashed our way straight in there. And there were four men inside.

'The leader of our squad, he was a right bastard, he wanted us to kill one each. The other lads all put a bullet in one of the Taliban guys. When they'd all done that, there was one left, and he was just a young boy, younger than me, sort of cowering in a corner. He was saying something to me, you know, kind of jabbering, and I couldn't understand what he was saying, obviously. And he was looking up at me and he had these big brown eyes and he was only a kid and I said, "I can't shoot him." I looked at the other guys and I was like, "I can't shoot him. There's no way I can shoot this kid. You can't make me do this. Please." But they did.'

Tears flowed down his cheeks unchecked. His eyes never left mine as he continued. 'Two days later we were all sent back to the UK. One of the lads was discharged and is now on civvy street, the other one's being sent somewhere else; the squad leader, well, he's army through and through, he'll be doing it for the rest of his life. Which just leaves me, really, who doesn't know whether he's coming or going. Now, in seven weeks' time I'm being sent to Iraq and I just don't know how I'm going to do it, I don't know how I can cope.'

I don't usually do this, but I stood from my chair, walked across to him and gave him a hug. It was all I could do to hold back the tears myself, and for a moment or so I reflected on the sheer senselessness of it all. Men at war. How many lives were ruined.

After comforting him for a few moments I took my seat again, taking more tissues from the box on my desk and leaning forward to hand them to him. He took them, thanking me, using them to dab at his eyes. His sad, tired, frightened eyes. I don't think I will ever forget the sight of them.

'You know what, Graham?' I said. 'I can tell you one thing that I know for sure, and that is that you are not going. Somehow, you're going to have a word with your commanding officer. I do not see you in Iraq. Don't ask me why, but I don't, darling.'

He looked at me. You know how I always say that each reading is like a little test of my ability, and this one, despite the incredibly emotional turn of events, had been no diffcrent. I had been able to show Graham evidence of the afterlife by passing messages from his grandfather and other relatives. Graham had been more than con-vinced that it was indeed his relatives I was talking to.

What I'm saying is that Graham believed.

But you know what? Even with all that evidence of my ability, when I told him that he would not be going to Iraq, what I saw in his face was disbelief. He was too polite to say so, of course, but I think that deep down he saw himself with that burden. He saw himself back in the army overseas.

The reading finished and we left my office. I have a screen that I use. I put it up when a reading begins and it screens off the door. It serves two purposes, really. Firstly, it stops any other guests from seeing in and stops the client from being distracted and seeing out. Secondly, it 'opens' me. When that screen goes across, something happens inside and I am open, and ready for business. I suppose that the screen is my little 'open' sign to spirit world. Now, I folded it up and moved it to one side, ushering Graham to the door, which I opened, letting him out into the hall. I reached the front door, opened it.

At that moment, John appeared. I think he'd been down the shop for a paper, or something like that, but he came walking up the drive and saw Graham, who, even though he had already stopped crying, now pulled himself up a little straighter, a sort of public face coming over him. You know what young guys are like. It was like he became all macho again.

Then he said to me, 'Just tell me, when I die will Granddad come for me?'

'Darling, he will,' I said. 'But don't worry, no one's going to shoot you, you're not going to die, you're not going to die like all those soldiers. Don't worry, darling, you're not.'

He and John shook hands and he left, walking down the drive and turning on to the road.

John and I watched him go.

'Who was that?' said John.

'That was a very, very troubled young man,' I said, still watching Graham as he got to the end of the road and went out of sight.

'Army, is it?'

'Yes, it was that friend of Fern's mate.'

'Oh, the one who went to Afghanistan?'

'Yes, that's the one. But he's not going back, you know.'

'No? Really? How do you know?'

'I don't know, darling,' I looked at John. 'I just do.'

Three days later, Graham was dead. He took a petrol-driven chainsaw and went into his mother's garage and got in his car. He sealed the car up then started the chainsaw. The car filled with carbon monoxide, killing him.

When they found him, the chainsaw was on the back seat, still running.

Graham's mother came to see me about a year later. The family had taken great comfort from the tape, she told me. This was the tape that all my clients are given after a reading.

I couldn't understand why. I was still slightly obsessed by the fact that I had missed his death.

'No,' said his mum, 'you are the most amazing person, you helped my son.'

I didn't know what to say. 'Well, you know, to be honest, I don't think I did help him ...'

She said, 'Oh, you did, to listen to the tape gives me so much comfort.'

'Why?'

'It's because you told him that he would be with his granddad. And I know how happy that would have made him.'

He had left a note explaining that he couldn't go to Iraq and couldn't live with what he had done in Afghanistan.

That reading represented something of a dilemma for me, because, for one of the first times in my career, I actually began to doubt my ability. There is a tendency for somebody in my position to wonder about where it all comes from and whether it might all suddenly disappear one day. Or perhaps it doesn't just 'suddenly' disappear.

Perhaps it gradually goes, it ebbs slowly away. It's always a worry. The reading with Graham made me so aware that it could simply be a fleeting thing.

In the end, I think what that reading proved to me was that I am simply not meant to see people's death before it has happened. The reading proved that my deal with him upstairs was being honoured.

Did he know he was about to kill himself when he came to see me? I've gone over and over our meeting, sifting through it, looking for clues like some kind of psychic I detective.

I think back to the look of disbelief that he gave me when I told him I didn't think he would be going to Iraq. Did I misinterpret that, perhaps? Was he looking at me wondering why I had not seen his death? Had his confidence in me been undermined?

I don't know, but I do think he was planning his suicide at the time of the reading. I was even more convinced of this after I'd spoken to his mum.

'You know, Sally,' she said to me, 'he had never spoken about the afterlife before. I mean, he was a young man, just twenty-three, he didn't really think about things like that. You don't, do you? Not at that age?'

I nodded my head, remembering how he did seem to be obsessed with the idea of spirit world; how many spirits had been round to speak to him.

'I don't really think he'd given it any thought before,' added his mum. 'I don't think he even really believed in the afterlife.'

'Well, he so wanted to be with his granddad,' I said. 'He wanted to know where he would go if he was killed on the battlefield. You know, it's not unusual for me to see people who are faced with their own imminent possible death, or for that person to become suddenly very interested in the idea of the afterlife. I mean, it is rare for me to see it with soldiers – frankly, I don't see a lot of soldiers – but I get a lot of people suffering from terminal diseases.'

It came to me then. Somehow, Graham had known he was going to die. Maybe, actually, I was wrong and he wasn't planning a suicide. But, somehow, he had some kind of precognitive sense that his fate was to die very soon. He had assumed it was to be on the battlefield. Yes, that would explain the look of disbelief when I told him he was not going to Iraq.

During the tour I did a show on Armistice Sunday, and I mentioned Graham to the audience. I didn't go into great detail, but I just said, 'You know, not all of our soldiers die because of where they are sent. They do not all die on the battlefield. There are some soldiers who come home and simply can't live with what they've done and what they've had to witness. They simply cannot live with themselves. So not only do we lose our soldiers on the battlefield, but we can lose them in other ways too. They can be scarred not just physically but mentally as well, and Graham was one of them. I just want you to know that I'm remembering him today.'

To be honest, it is one of those readings I'll probably dwell upon for the rest of my days. I hope that when I eventually move across to spirit world, I am able to meet up with Graham once again, to give him another hug.

One thing I do know is that when I see him he will be

happy and in a better place, where he will be free of hatred and war and racism and all the silly, petty, religious and political struggles he was asked to help fight for.

And I know this too: he'll be with his granddad.

Thirty-two

Abortions and miscarriages

I am an advocate of the woman's right to abort a pregnancy if she does not want a baby, I truly am. A woman's body is her own. And you're dealing with human error and human frailty. A woman needs to be able to make that choice if she so desires.

Something I am asked an awful lot is about the spirits of babies who have been aborted, or those lost via miscarriage. The question is, *Does it have a spirit?*

The answer is that some do. I have a lot of women who come to me with this issue on their mind. I can pick up pregnancies, so it stands to reason that I will be able to pick up abortions, too, and I often find myself saying to a woman, 'Oh, you've got three children?'

She might say 'No.' But I can see that look in her eyes. 'Why?' she'll say.

I know. That's the point at which I know, and I'll say, 'You've had a termination then.'

And the amount of times – oh my goodness – that she'll say, 'Yes, but my husband doesn't know about it . . .'

If I had a pound for every time that has happened, well, I'd probably be able to afford to live in Fulham.

So, the next question is, if I am picking up on them, am

I then picking up a spirit? Because if am, then it stands to reason that an aborted baby has a spirit, doesn't it?

The answer is no, I don't necessarily see an aborted soul. What I'm picking up on is the journey, the life, of the person sitting in front of me.

So, no, I don't see the spirit of the child, of the foetus. I call it the pregnancy. I don't see the spirit or soul of the pregnancy, which I think is very reassuring for a lot of people who come to see me.

The only time it isn't is when people are desperate for children and every time they conceive they miscarry. However, in these cases I usually do see a miscarried soul, and I think that this has something to do with the strength of desire for the baby.

Recently I read for a woman and said, 'There are three little girls here in spirit; three little female souls.'

'Oh,' she said, 'that's because I've had three babies. I lost three babies. I never knew what they were – the sex, I mean. Oh my goodness, were they girls?'

It's funny, it's almost as if the souls of those babies who miscarried somehow stayed around their mother on earth plane, whereas an aborted pregnancy does not.

I get girls who come to see me who got pregnant and didn't want the baby, normally because they're no longer with the man. So they had a termination. Most of the time I do not see the pregnancy in spirit, but there are times that I do, and it will really shock the person who has come to see me. To be honest, it's the last thing I want to do, to see a pregnancy in spirit like that, because I don't want to make the person feel guilty about the decision they've made. But, like I say, I do not interpret, I rarely change the messages I am given and it is no different on these occasions.

At the end of the day, no decision about a termination will ever be taken lightly – well, I hope not anyway, certainly not if I'm talking about those who come to see me – and there will always be so much worry and potential guilt involved. They don't call it soul-searching for nothing. I think it can be very tough for a lot of people.

But even a miscarriage pales into insignificance when you consider the sheer heartache caused by the death of a child.

Thirty-three

The worst pain of all

The first thing I would like to say about the death of a child is that it appears to everybody that it is the wrong way round. How can a child go first?

Years and years ago, my youngest, Fern, was very, very ill with osteomyelitis.

I went through it in my last book, but to cut a long and very painful story short, it all happened one afternoon when Fern was complaining of pain in her leg. At the time, I didn't take her particularly seriously – I even took her shopping – but things became so bad, and she was obviously in so much pain, that I ended up rushing her to hospital, where she was diagnosed with a very rare bone condition called osteomyelitis.

The night she went into hospital, she lay in bed, and it was touch and go. I stayed with her all night and, as I sat with her, not even able to touch her because she was in so much pain, with a fan just behind us keeping her cool, do you know what I did?

I prayed to God.

I prayed for him to give me osteomyelitis, not her; to take it from her and give it to me; that the very next day when I awoke it would be me dying, not her.

And I know full well that I'm not the first mother to

offer up such a prayer. In fact, I would go further and say that *most* mums would do the very same thing.

There's nothing you wouldn't do. Which means that when the unthinkable happens, the pain of bereavement is magnified a hundredfold.

Every parent I have ever spoken to who has had a child die has been wracked with guilt on some level or another. If it isn't, 'Oh, it should have been me, they were only little, I've had a life,' then it's 'Did I take care of them enough? Could I have done something to prevent it?'

I had one woman who came to see me once with a dreadful story – her son had died in a fight. He had banged his head on the kerb and died. What she kept saying to me was, 'Why did I let him go out that night? I didn't want him to go out.'

The thing is, we think of excuses. We think of excuses for what we should have done. We wonder. We wish we had done things differently. We torture ourselves with thoughts of what might have been.

And basically, at the end of the day, it boils down to the fact that we want to take on that death. We want our child's death to have happened to us.

It's that simple.

So the first hurdle that I find I have to get over before talking about the spiritual side when it concerns child death is the guilt. In a weird kind of way we feel a shame that we live and our child is dead. Then, of course, there is the anger. It follows the usual pattern of grieving, really, only writ large. Because child death seems so unjust, parents often respond to it with a great rage. Say if the child has been in hospital, then nine times out of ten parents will direct their blame at the medical staff, or the NHS, or the government. Because, in my experience, disease – well, cancer – is the most common killer of children. A lot of children die of leukaemia. Then you get young adults, especially boys in their early twenties, who die in car crashes. Then, and it pains me to say this, it really does, but murder is fast becoming one of the ways in which children are being killed.

It's a horrible thing to have to point out, but more and more mums come to me whose child has been killed in a fight, or been stabbed, or been beaten up. Of course, it's always for the most trivial, senseless reasons: arguments over girls and mobile phones, and silly disputes over territory where one thinks face has been lost.

Now if you can imagine the kind of anger that would be directed at, say, a hospital, then triple, *quadruple* that, to arrive at the sense of injustice parents feel when their child has been murdered. The difference is that in the former instance their rage is directed somewhere. With a murder, all too often the anger can fly off at the most dangerous angles.

Then imagine if your child dies in a car accident. You'd feel guilt *and* anger, wouldn't you? If it wasn't your child driving, there is anger at the person who was. If there was more than one person in the car, you can bet your life that one of them has survived ... So, again, more frustration and anger.

A word that brilliantly sums all of this up is sorrow. Parents are completely and utterly immersed in it; they feel they have nowhere to turn.

I don't think there is another form of death that can hit

anyone as hard as losing a child, I really don't. I mean, I'm close to John, you're close to your other half. And if my John was to die or your other half was to die, then of course you would be absolutely devastated. But I have to say – and I would say this to John's face (he's going to read it in here anyway) – if I lost one of my kids, the grief I felt over that death would far outweigh the grief of losing John. It just would. I don't know what I'd do, I'd go completely mad. There are a lot of people who simply can't take it, but to them I have the same thing to say that I said to a lady the other day:

'You do know that it is very important that you're still here, don't you?'

She just stared at me with a blank look. 'What do you mean?'

'Because while you are here on earth plane, you keep your son's name alive. You keep him alive because you're here.'

She looked at me. Something unreadable in that look. However, I knew what was going on beneath.

'I know why you're here,' I told her. 'I know exactly why you're here, darling.'

'Why is that, Sally?' she said, her voice very, very small in the room.

'You're here because you're thinking about killing yourself, aren't you?' I said.

'Yes, Sally,' she said.

And then she broke down. 'I just wanted to join my son,' she said. 'I want to be with him, you don't know what it is like. You just don't know . . .'

I find it very difficult in situations like that. I knew

totally where she was coming from. It's not that I have ever lost a child – God forbid – but I knew exactly where she was coming from, I could feel her pain.

And it's at times like that I really have to trust spirit world. If I have a mother who has come to see me and they are considering killing themselves, then logic dictates that by confirming to them the existence of an afterlife I am in fact increasing the likelihood that they will go through with it.

Does that make sense? If I tell them there is an after-life, it's like saying, 'You have more chance of seeing your child very soon.' And what you have to remember is that this is what they want. It is *all* they want.

That woman sat in front of me in my house that day, and she was a broken person. A truly shattered individual. She had known the love of her child, which is to know the greatest force there is on earth plane. It is more powerful than any drug, stronger than any faith. It is a force so monumentally strong it is almost frightening.

In short, I don't think there is anything you wouldn't do for that love. Taking your own life is nothing. And I understand that instinct. It's yet another of the instances when I need to trust in spirit to give me the right messages, and that if there really was the chance she was going to kill herself, then the messages would be different.

Death is so personal to each person. I always think of it as being comparable to being present at a complete stranger's birth. It's at different ends of the spectrum, but it's on that level. To sit with a parent and be a part of the grief over their child dying, I really believe that nothing could be more private.

It means we have to form quite a bond. When you think about it, it is very, very hard for a mum and dad to sit with someone like me, because they know they are going to hear things they simply do not want to hear. Much of this will be for purposes of validation. For example, the parents of the murder victim, Sarah, heard some very gruesome and upsetting details of their daughter's death that were given to me in order to establish authenticity.

It is almost as though I am being sensational with these people, when my instinct is to do the opposite. After all, what I do is not a circus act, and I don't like to see it treated as such. It is very serious and it deals with real human emotions.

Just as an aside, you might think that seeing clients on tour was much more difficult than seeing them in my office for that very reason. But I think it works in a theatre because people in the audience are very respectful of who you are speaking to, and in a way become privy to something that usually only I ever see. And that is a bonus. Put it another way, you will never get the chance to see a psychic at work in his or her office. On tour, you do. And most people are very, very respectful of that, too. And when people come to see me, they are not coming just for a reading. They are also coming to see me in action; to have an insider's glimpse of what goes on when a medium sees her client. That makes for a very interesting atmosphere in the theatre. Most of the time, when I'm dealing with really sensitive issues, such as child death, you could hear a pin drop in the auditorium, and when spirits come through and begin passing on messages, and people in the audience know they are communicating with their loved ones – and their children on the other side – well, that is a very humbling experience. It blows people away.

Now, here is something interesting. Sometimes I might have a mother who has lost her child at birth and I can see the child, and he or she is four years old. Yet, the mother is coming to see me ten years after the child's death.

Isn't that weird? You have three aspects there. A stillborn baby, which is how the soul passed over. It passed over ten years ago. Yet the spirit is four years old.

Now, this is what I have worked out: that many babies who die as babies grow until the next sibling is born.

In this one particular instance, I said to the woman, 'Well, he's four years old.'

She said, 'No, that's impossible, he was stillborn.'

I said, 'Yes, but he's appearing to me aged four years old. And I know what you're going to say next . . .'

'It happened ten years ago.'

She was shaking her head. This wasn't making sense to her at all, I could see that. 'Surely he would be aged ten?'

'Wait a minute,' I said. 'Was your next baby born four years later?'

'Yes,' she said, 'yes, you're right. How did you know that?'

'I know it because he stopped growing when the next baby was born. Why this is, I don't know, but it happens many, many, many times.'

It's absolutely incredible, isn't it? Child spirits grow in the afterlife. I saw a woman in her seventies once, and I said to her, 'I've got a young man here of twenty-two, he says his name is Paul.'

'Oh,' she said, 'that's my son.'

'Well, I'm so sorry, darling,' I said.

She said, 'No, don't worry, it was a long time ago. He was seven when he died.'

Yet here I am seeing him aged twenty-two; what is all that about then?

Then, on the other hand, I get people who have had a stillborn baby, and the stillborn baby is there. And not too long ago I spoke to a lady whose ten-week-old baby had died. I can't tell you how upsetting that was, she was in bits.

I got the baby's name, that it was a little girl. The mother was in her fifties by now and do you know how the baby appeared? No, not grown up, as some of the others do. This one came through in the arms of a relative of theirs, literally a babe in arms. I got the name of the relative, too.

I said, 'She's holding a baby up,' and I lifted my arms up to illustrate.

There was a particular way that the relative in spirit was holding the baby, that made me want to demonstrate it to the mother.

True to form, this was the spirit world giving me a message, because the mother jumped, her eyes widening, glistening wet with tears.

'And that was how they held her up to me,' she said, clearly shocked. She understood completely.

Now, I don't want you to go away thinking that there's anything strange about all this, because there isn't. Not everything is how we think it should be, and even though some babies grow and some babies don't, we have to trust that there is a reason for that. Just because we do not know what the reason is, does not mean it doesn't exist. We have to trust.

A question I'm regularly asked is if children in spirit are different to adult spirits. The answer to that is a very definite *no*. I also have a lot of people who worry that if the child was very young when he or she died, that their soul is going to come back to earth.

They don't, not unless they are evil, and babies are never evil. Remember, the soul is poisoned by the mind and body to make it evil, so babies are never evil, and will never be recycled in that way. Neither, just because they're so young, are they prevented from communicating with us on earth plane. I get the information from them in exactly the same way as I do from adult spirits, in a kind of thought process. Just the same way I would get it from a dog, even.

I always get a ripple of laughter when I talk about a dog 'saying' something, which I am not offended by, but what I do say is that what you have to try and understand – and it's going to sound mad – is that I'm getting this information 'beamed' into my head and it is the dog which is 'speaking'.

That's all very well if we're talking about a dog, but the baby spirit wouldn't have sophisticated thoughts, would it? It does, yes, because the soul is adult, remember? In other words, the spirit who has passed as a baby is exactly the same as the spirit who has passed at 101.

They don't behave like 101-year-olds, though. I think what happens is that a lot of babies will give childlike signs because the parent has to know it's a young one, even though in spirit it's not really a baby, it's a soul.

What I find is that a lot of children in spirit leave what you might call babyish signs. I get an awful lot of parents who will say things such as, 'I heard her crying last night, I'm sure I did.' And to that I would say, 'This is perfectly logical. Their spirit wants you to have validation of their presence in spirit world. Although the soul is capable of communicating to you in much the same way as I am now, what point would there be in that? You need confirmation of the spirit as "your daughter".'

Other signs will include toys being placed in certain places, disappearing, or being moved. It's important for parents to look out for all of these signs at a time of bereavement.

Still, though, sometimes there can literally be no consoling those who are left behind. Let me tell you a story . . .

Thirty-four

Healing the hardest hurt

She came to the house, the lady. She wasn't crying but she was very, very quiet. I had no clue as to why she had come.

I introduced myself and we stepped into my office. She took a seat and I busied myself with the screen, opening it up across the door.

As I did so, I could feel myself open and knew one thing straight away. This was to do with the death of a child. A knowing. A psychic knowing? Perhaps. After all, it could have been the death of her husband. Certainly, she seemed as though she was a person who was in mourning.

The next thing I knew, just as surely as I knew my own name, was *this is going to be really, really hard.*

You must remember that, of the people who come to see me, about half come with concerns involving romance or finances or their career or something else that you might consider quite mundane or day-to-day. The other half come to see me with issues involving death. Of those, most hope to contact adult spirits, and most of those will have passed over some time ago.

That leaves those who come hoping to contact the spirits of children, and they are in a thankfully small minority. Those who come to contact the spirit of a child who has only just passed over? Well, I'm very happy to say that they are in an even smaller minority.

But I have seen thousands and thousands of people over the years, which means I have dealt with hundreds and hundreds of children who have passed over and they are always difficult; they are always the hardest reading of the day. And I've been doing this long enough to get a feeling about them. This one, I had a feeling about. I had the sense that the spirit was a recent one. I also knew that this would be a hard reading. It was with a certain amount of trepidation that I took my seat opposite the woman, smiled, and began talking, the usual speech.

As I spoke, I took her in. She had a certain bearing. I could tell that she came from a wealthy background. Or certainly that she had money behind her now. Her clothes were well-cut and her make-up expensive and beautifully applied. There was a sense of her mourning, but that she was stoic about it.

There was a pause when I had finished explaining my work to her. Then I said, 'You've lost a child, haven't you?'

A tear fell from one of her eyes and made its way down her face. For a moment or so I thought she was going to do nothing about it. Then more tears. Then she reached to dab her eyes.

'Was he seven years old?' I asked.

She didn't answer. Instead, sniffing slightly, she leant forward and reached for her handbag, which she had placed at her feet. She brought the handbag to her lap, opened it and took from it a photograph that she passed to me.

I reached for it. Looked at it. It was a photograph of two boys, one a two-year-old and one a seven-year-old.

In that instant I knew it was the younger boy, not the seven-year-old.

'That's the one,' I said, indicating the little boy in the photograph. 'It was him, wasn't it, darling?'

'Yes,' she managed.

'He's here,' I said.

And that was it. She broke down, and for a moment the reading was temporarily suspended as she tried to gather her emotions and I handed her tissues.

I thought, actually, that we might have to to suspend it altogether, as she was quite literally inconsolable for some considerable length of time. After a while, she began to calm down, and we resumed. Of course, during the time she was crying, I was still picking things up about her son.

When she was able to continue talking, I said to her, 'Why is he doing this on his chest?' And I reached to my chest and pushed my hand against it.

This set her off once again. My heart reached out to her, it really did. All I could do was try to comfort and console her as she struggled to gather her emotions.

Still I had this sense of the spirit and there being something wrong with his chest. Then, it came to me. As she nodded, giving me validation, the pictures began to form in my head and the tragedy of it made me catch my breath.

Oh God, this beautiful, beautiful little boy.

It happened one afternoon. He was aged two and had

wanted a cup of a hot drink. He didn't want it in his normal cup, he wanted it in a grown-up's cup, so she had made him this hot drink and – like any good mother – she had put it on the worktop to let it cool down considerably before she gave it to him. But he had gone over to the worktop and grabbed the cup. He must have had a stool, or he had stood on a drawer, but somehow he was able to reach up to the worktop and grab the cup, which he pulled from the worktop and on top of himself. The hot drink had gone all down his front, burning him.

She took him straight to the hospital, where they confirmed that the burn was not too serious – not third-degree burns – and the little boy was discharged.

It would have been OK. The burn wasn't that serious. The problem was that the hospital let him out too soon.

He came home and soon developed a very high temperature.

Then she rang the doctor. The doctor told her, 'Oh, that's just because it's a burn. Give him some more Calpol and he'll be fine.'

She did as she was directed. You do, don't you? You trust doctors.

The next day he still wasn't well, so she took him to another doctor, who told her, 'He'll be OK, it's just because it's a burn.'

He was given some other tablets and sent home.

At home he seemed to get worse, and she fretted about whether or not to ring the doctor again, thinking about how two doctors now had told there was nothing to worry about, concerned at being thought of as wasting the doctors' time, all the stuff that goes through your head at a time like that ...

He died. He died in her arms of toxic shock.

For some moments after all this came to me, I thought, *oh no, I simply cannot cope with this; I'm not going to be able to work after this.*

There were so many aspects of the little boy's death that cut through me. For a start, the little boy looked very much like my own grandson. Also, just the way he had died. It seemed so unfair, so arbitrary.

I suppose that in many ways what I felt was a reduced version of what his own parents had gone through.

The little boy was with me in spirit, and he was such a beautiful little thing, who so desperately wanted to bring some comfort to his mother. The funniest thing, he was telling me that she was going to have another child.

He was quite insistent, the little scamp.

But I just couldn't bring myself to do it. Here was his mother, in bits, mourning his death. I could not find the words to say to her that she was going to have another one. I mean, the last thing you want to say to a mother who has lost her child is, 'You can have another one.' How cruel would that be? It's a bit like saying to somebody who's just lost a loved one, 'Never mind, plenty more fish in the sea.'

I just couldn't do it. For some time I had this to and fro in my head. The little boy, he was desperate for me to tell this to his mother. But I had her there in front of me, I could see the state she was in.

I felt like saying to him, 'Come on, look at her. I cannot possibly say this. She's missing you far too much.

We have to let her grieve for you before she can look to the future.' But he'd kept on insisting that I say something. In the end I had to abide by my code. I have used it for years and years, and it has rarely let me down, so I fell back on it then.

'I've got something to say to you, darling,' I said to her, keeping my voice as gentle as possible. 'Can you bear to listen to me?'

She dabbed her eyes with a tissue, the way women do when they're wearing eye makeup and they don't want to spoil it.

'Do you know what he's telling me now, darling?' I said.

She shook her head, no.

'Well,' I said, 'you're going to have to forgive me, but I may never see you again, so I have to tell you: you're going to have another baby.'

Again, it was one of those moments where I really felt that I had lost the reading. Like I had passed through belief to the other side, to disbelief. Because she was shaking her head, still wiping her eyes, still snuffling back the tears.

But very definitely shaking her head.

'Absolutely not,' she managed. 'I will never have any more children.'

I said, 'I can understand you saying that, darling, but do you know what? I know that you are going to have a surprise because your son is here telling me that, and I believe him, don't you?'

'No,' she said. 'No, not this time, Sally, it's just not going to happen.'

I couldn't argue with that.

'Does he think it was my fault?' she asked me, later in the reading.

The spirit I saw with her seemed to shimmer slightly. Angrily, as though the very idea had offended it. Into my head came the thought that . . .

'No, darling, not at all. He says it was one of those things. He says that he is very, very happy in spirit world.'

It was an incredibly emotional reading, and she went away . . . well, quite frankly, she went away a complete wreck. What would you expect? I mean, she left, having taken messages from her tiny little boy on the other side; having been told she was going to have another child, and she didn't believe that for a second.

On top of that, she had told me that she was having problems in her marriage.

This happens an awful lot when a child dies. In my experience, actually, very, very few relationships can survive that kind of trauma; divorce is extremely commonplace in such situations.

I have been able to help in certain instances, and definitely a good medium can help couples to solve their differences – you would be amazed what great marriage counsellors we can be. Happily, this was one such situation. The next time I saw her she came up with her husband. It was the anniversary of the child's death and during that difficult year they had had very little in the way of a relationship. He had closed down and didn't really want to know her. I think the problem was that, deep down, he blamed her for leaving the hot drink on the side.

Through spirit world, and through their little boy on the other side, I was able to reassure him that it wasn't her fault; that their little boy didn't think it was her fault either.

He repeated his message that it was just 'one of those things'. That was what he said, those exact words. He said, 'She was always such a great mum. She always had so much time for me. She was always doing her best.'

I like to think that his messages did them a great deal of good. They didn't go away laughing and giggling, like two young lovers, but I think he definitely began to understand a little more about what had happened that day. I think he learnt to let go of the blame.

'I'm playing with my toys,' he told them.

Father was, of course, slightly sceptical, but I named one of the toys, something very, very distinctive.

I said, 'He's showing me that you are sitting on his bed in his room.'

'Oh my God,' she said, putting her hands to her face, the image triggering something inside her.

'He's showing me that you're sitting on his bed in his room and you're holding something. It's like a dog. Did he have a soft brown dog?'

She was nodding now, her eyes as wide as saucers above her fingertips, staring at me as though she could not believe what I was saying. It's a common enough reaction. People come wanting to believe but there is a moment when they really do – not when they believe, but when they *know* – and it is always quite something to see.

'He's showing me a soft brown dog, a teddy bear.'

She was nodding still.

'He always held it, it has large ears. He's telling me that he still has it. Why is he telling me that he still has it?'

She took her hand away from her face. 'Because I put it in his coffin.'

That is something I get a lot. People place items in a coffin and the spirit tells me that they still have it. And this brings me on, actually, to something else I need to discuss regarding the grieving process. How do you cope with those things your loved one leaves behind? I want to talk about that next.

Before I do, though, there's one last thing to say about that couple and their little boy in spirit.

They came back a few weeks later to tell me that they were expecting a baby.

Thirty-five

Bereavement and instinct

Firstly, my feeling on this is that we cannot give ourselves too much responsibility – we cannot clutter our lives with the possessions of somebody who has passed over. It's something I'm asked about a lot, though, especially by women, funnily enough.

I spoke to a lady not long ago, for example, who said to me, 'I've got all his shoes. He had pairs and pairs of shoes and he loved them. What do I do, Sally?'

'Well,' I said, 'did he have a favourite pair of shoes?'

'Oh, yes, certainly. He was a big one for favourites. He had a favourite pair of shoes and a favourite jacket . . .'

'Oh well,' I said, 'keep those forever. Fold them up, put them away. If it's a jacket, you could leave it hanging in your cupboard, just at the end there.'

She looked surprised, as though she had expected me to advise her simply to dispose of all his belongings, and to be honest it wouldn't be *wrong* to do that, just that my feeling is, why not keep them?

I said as much to the woman. 'You know, we tend to keep items of jewellery, and it's usually the son who will get the watch, that's a bit of a tradition. But I think at the end of the day we should abide, not so much by tradition, but more by our own inner feelings. We should trust our sixth sense.'

This is such a big thing with me. I really feel that we should listen to that little inner voice more and more. I call it the sixth sense as you know, but you might also call it your gut instinct, a feeling you can't quite get rid of. That is the feeling you have to listen to.

Shortly, I will talk about reading messages from the other side, but the first step is to identify what those messages might be. I definitely see the sixth sense as being intrinsically linked to spirit world. What I'm saying is, if your sixth sense tells you to save his favourite jacket in the cupboard, then perhaps that is your husband in spirit asking you to keep the jacket.

Another time, I had someone come to see me who had her mother's cardigan. This cardigan was falling to bits, full of holes.

'I have to keep it in a freezer bag,' she said to me. 'Do you think it's about time I threw it away?' .

I said, 'Well, how do you feel about that?'

'Well, I just think it holds memories of her.'

'Don't ever get rid of it then, love,' I said. 'Let the people around you know how you feel about it.'

There again, I really felt that her mother in spirit wanted her to hold on to that cardigan. For what reason, I don't know and could not possibly say. Maybe it had some kind of talismanic significance for her.

I think using your sixth sense, your instinct, your gut feeling – whatever you want to call it – is absolutely vital in the aftermath of the death of a loved one, I really do. We as a society have certain traditions we feel we must adhere to, certain modes of behaviour. And because when a loved one dies we go into a kind of autopilot mode, it can be very easy to follow these dictates without really thinking about it, and thus ignoring our gut feeling.

Try not to do that, is my advice – in all aspects of your life, actually, but especially during a period of bereavement.

If what I say is right – and I believe it to be so – then the feelings you have are being communicated to you directly from spirit world and it is vital that you listen to them. Even if it seems a bit off-the-wall at the time, or if relatives and friends are advising you otherwise.

Remember, also, that listening to one's instinct is a form of trust. It's trusting yourself. Take another example. You're driving home, the same route as usual, even though there are probably three or four roads you could take to get you there.

Then, all of a sudden, you're going down that familiar road and you think, 'I'm going to go a different way today,' and you do – you follow your instincts. You can almost always guarantee that it will be confirmed to you that you did the right thing. You will hear that there was an accident, or the road was closed, or that something had just happened, or was about to happen.

If you didn't listen to your instinct, then you'd be stuck in traffic and you'd be thinking, 'Do you know what? I knew I shouldn't have come this way. I knew I should've gone the other way.' Your instinct confirms to you that you did the right thing. How many times have you been sitting in a queue of traffic and sighed, 'I knew we should have gone the other way.' Or, 'I had a *feeling* we should have gone the other way.'

You say it without even thinking about it, don't you? You say: 'I had a *feeling* that ...' and you did, you really did.

Somewhere, deep down, you had a feeling and you didn't listen to it at that moment. Trusting your sixth sense is a matter of listening to those feelings, and in order to do that it's a question of recognizing them and excavating them from deep down inside yourself.

If you're always a slave to social conventions and 'common sense' and other people's ideas of right and wrong, you might find it more difficult to do this. Not impossible. Don't get me wrong, I'm not saying you should start rejecting conventional morality or anything like that. That's not my style.

What I am saying, though, is don't be blindly led by these things at the expense of other signals you are being given. In this case, the evidence of your instinct.

I think if you take one lesson away from this book regarding spirit world and the processes of grieving and bereavement and how we can benefit from those in the afterlife, then that lesson should be: *listen*.

Because if you don't listen, you will never hear.

OK, so let's define instinct. What are you looking for? Where do you find this voice you need to heed?

Say if you were offered two jobs and you were discussing the two jobs with your other half, who said to you, 'What does your instinct say?' How would you find your instinct?

Well, it's a feeling, because instinct often kicks in when

logic is saying do one thing, and the instinct is saying the opposite. When, inside, you feel tension between two opposing choices, even though one seems more logical.

So, in that two jobs example, you could look at both jobs and you could know that job A pays more money and is easier to get to and you know somebody who works there. So to all intents and purposes, you should take job A, shouldn't you? But inside there's something nagging at you, that little alarm bell.

It may not be a conscious voice, but it's there. That's your instinct talking. That's your psychic valve (I'll come to the psychic valve soon, I promise). It's your psychic valve vibrating.

In the same way, you choose a different route on the journey home. Why not take the normal road, when you take it every night and it's the most convenient route? Why not? Because you listened to the little bell which was jangling, telling you to take a different road. And you know what I think? That you should always listen to that instinct. Take that different route home. Take job B. Listen to your instinct because that's spirit world sending you messages.

The difficulty, of course, comes in identifying that nagging feeling as instinct or, when the nagging feeling isn't particularly strong, then listening to it. We all know that sometimes 'instinct kicks in' and will override all rational thought. It's when the alarm bell isn't so much ringing as just tinkling that you have to listen hardest.

And I suppose that now I should talk about the valve.

Thirty-six

The valve

Spirits are around us all of the time. It's seeing them, that's the thing. I've touched upon how I think my childhood and my home at Waldemar is what helped shape my ability – how I can see spirits – and this is why I developed my theory of the valve.

Now, promise to stay with me on this one, because it might sound a bit nuts at first.

I believe we all have what I think of as a little valve in our head, which opens and closes. For instance, have you ever had the experience of thinking about somebody then when the phone rings that person is on the other end of the line? What about you and your partner thinking of the same thing at the same time? Strange coincidences? A feeling of déjà vu?

These are psychic moments, instances when we are using our latent psychic ability – maybe without even knowing it. At a time like that, during a psychic moment, the valve is open and there is an energy in our head, a psychic energy, a sixth sense.

And then the valve closes.

The valve, I suppose, represents belief. Or the potential for belief.

Me, because of my background, my valve stays open.

This, I think, is because the spirits met me at a very young age. Because when we're younger we have this innocence, don't we? We're not polluted by facts and reasoning. We have no knowledge of logic. Our minds are open.

Because of this our sixth sense is ripe for development. There is nothing stopping it, you see. No preconceptions about what is possible and what is impossible, of this world or the next one. The mind can fly.

Which is what my mind did, on a daily basis. For me, that little internal valve in my head was open all of the time in what I thought was an abnormal way. Years and years later when I was tested by Dr Gary Schwartz, and we discussed my theory of the valve, he said to me, 'Well, why does it have to be abnormal? Perhaps that is how we are evolving?'

I thought for a moment, wondering what he meant. Because if my theory was correct, then it was the process of reaching maturity and adulthood that closed the valve. If mine was open, did that mean I was somehow in a state of arrested development, lagging behind the rest of the adult world?

'Well,' he said, 'how about reversing that? Perhaps one day all of us will have it. You've just got there before everyone else.'

Perhaps you're the mother or father of young children, and your child is asking you about ghosts. A good mum or dad would say, 'Don't worry, there are no such things as ghosts.'

Now, I'm not saying my mum and dad were no good, but my mum, definitely, never made any attempt to close my valve. Perhaps this was as a result of being Nanny Gladys's daughter. It made her a believer.

So certainly when it came to parental input, my valve stayed open. Outside the home there would have been people telling me, 'Don't be so bloody silly, girl,' but at home, where it really counted, the spirit world was allowed free passage into my head.

And that's where it started, I believe. No, I don't think for a second that the same would have happened to any child. What I reckon is that it was a classic case of being the right person in the right place at the right time; some kind of strange psychic confluence.

It must have been, because when you think about it, not everyone in Waldemar saw the ghosts. Not my sister Gina, for example. Presumably her valve was also open. She had that potential. But she didn't have that extra 'thing' that I do. The thing being – well, I don't call it my 'gift' and I never call it 'power'. If somebody describes it as a 'gift', well, thank you very much, but it's not really the way I choose to describe it. The way I see it is more in terms of something that I have developed, a muscle. If you work an arm muscle every day your arm will look different to somebody who doesn't. It will be a different shape, more defined.

And that's what I believe happens with the sixth sense. I think my valve opened up, and because of some innate 'something' inside of me, my sixth sense began to work and develop and grow.

My sister, on the other hand – her valve may well have been open but she didn't have that same innate ability that I have, so her sixth sense was never worked. That ability never developed.

Compare it to being able to play a musical instrument, for example. There are plenty of people who can play the piano. There are fewer people capable of keeping an audience rapt. Even fewer who can demonstrate genuine genius at the piano. Don't get me wrong, I'm not claiming to be some kind of psychic maestro, and certainly not a genius. But if you put a child with musical ability into a house filled with music then you'd expect to see that ability develop. I think the same thing happened to me with my sixth sense.

Sometimes, it blows my mind to think of it. You could be a person open to spirit world, your valve well and truly open, but who lives in a modern house, with down-to-earth parents, so that ability won't ever get the chance to develop.

You could be a person who lives in – for want of a better term – a haunted house, but whose valve is closed. Again, your sixth sense might go no further.

Spirit world must have wanted me, though. It must have done. Because I truly believe that someone orchestrates all this. I think that there must hundreds of thousands, no, *millions* of people whose valves are open like mine. For whatever reason, though, that sense they have is not allowed to fly, to sing, to develop. Think of the pianist or the violinist: you see a true virtuoso at work and he or she will seem at one with their instrument.

I'll give you an example. The other night, I was watching violinist Nigel Kennedy in concert on TV and, goodness, he was incredible. What I realized was that there must be millions who can play the violin to his standard, yet can't get the same sound out of the instrument.

There is a reason that this man and his violin work so well together, some kind of chemistry.

When I watched Nigel Kennedy playing his violin, I'm not kidding you, his music came from somewhere inside him. Like anybody else who can play the same instrument, he knows, technically, how to play at you, but that didn't matter. His music was coming from inside of him. It was his soul talking.

So, how does he do it? Well, I suppose what he does is to somehow forget what he can do, making it second nature. He forgets what he can do and instead concentrates on what he *is*. Instead of playing the piece of music, he channels it.

Which is what I do. And, in a way, that's what I have with spirit world.

Again, no, I'm not trying to claim I'm the Nigel Kennedy of mediums. I haven't got the crazy hair, for a start. What I'm saying is that it's a case of the right person finding their strength.

Your valve has to be open. You have to have the ability. You have to have something inside of you. Of course, with me, I consciously have to open and afterwards I consciously close down. But somewhere in between I'm no longer Sally Morgan. There is no conscious mind. If I am open to spirit world then I'm not playing the song, I am channelling it.

A sceptic will claim that they don't believe in spirits and that my scenario is rubbish, because it would never happen. But that is because of their valve. Their valve simply isn't open. Spirits are not drawn towards them. If I walk into a house that has a spirit I am much more likely to see that spirit because my ability is so heightened. I am a magnetic pole for spirits and, not only am I very well known on earth plane, I'm very well known to spirit world. I am the doorway between earth plane and spirit world and, as a result, spirits are drawn towards me. I have an analogy to that. Imagine an old radio. You know you used to have to tune your radio? Before the days of digital radios, this was. Well, I'm a bit like that. When I go on stage it is as though I am tuning in to spirit world. The noise I hear in my head is very similar actually, it's the noise of many different voices trying to make themselves heard. Then, after a bit of fiddling around on the dial, perfect. Crystal clear. And that's when I am talking to spirit world. Because I am this doorway.

Do you know what I think? That the day will come when we actually, scientifically, label that sixth sense – this valve I'm talking about – and give it a scientific term, a meaning; something that is recognized not just by believers, but by everybody.

I truly believe this, and I so hope I am around to see it happen, maybe even be one of those who helps to make it happen, for it is my ultimate ambition to open some kind of centre or retreat in order to explore my ability more fully, both in myself, but, more importantly, in others.

When you think about it, just look at Darwin. He completely upset the Church when he developed his theory of evolution, which contradicted something we'd believed for centuries – that the earth was created in seven days. Yet now Darwin's theories are accepted as scientific fact and it is possible to have a belief in God as well as a belief in Darwinism. I mean, I don't think the two are mutually exclusive.

In the same way, I think that you can have a belief in spirituality and have that run parallel with a faith in the ways of science. That's me, though, and I feel I'm something of a lone voice when it comes to this theory.

Maybe one day, though, eh? A girl can dream. I don't think it's too far-fetched to believe that one day my theories may be accepted by the establishment. Who knows, just as we talk of Darwin's theory of evolution now, perhaps one day we will talk of Sally Morgan's theory of the valve? I'm only pulling your leg. (Well, half pulling it.)

It will probably never happen, of course, because I also believe that the reason so much of spirit world and the afterlife remains mysterious is part of some divine plan. I think it is God's will that the two disciplines of spirituality and science do not co-exist. For if science were to embrace spirituality then, quite quickly, the spirituality side of things would be phased out, and he does not want that.

The reason is that scientists work to find answers to things that spirituality says have no rational explanation. You could almost say it is the scientist's job to deny any existence of a higher power.

On the other hand, those with faith tend to be very mistrustful of science. Never the twain shall meet.

So it is my theory that if we were ever to come up with a scientific explanation for this phenomenon, then the scientific community would use that explanation to undermine spirituality. And you know what? God does not want that. Him upstairs, he does not want us in denial of his presence.

Therefore, it is my belief that God could never allow us to have a scientific explanation for this, because he is not a scientist.

This is about the soul – and the soul cannot be categorized and rationalized and explained.

Thirty-seven

Our psychic pets

This sixth sense I'm talking about is even more prevalent in dogs. We used to have a dog and it would stand in the front room. This was when John was working, and I would know John was on his way home because the dog would suddenly jump on the sofa and start barking.

Amazing. How on earth would the dog know that?

John wasn't coming home at the same time every night, yet the dog knew precisely when John was about to drive around the corner on his way home. He would jump up and start barking *before* John turned into the road.

That's just one example of that animal sixth sense at work, and in fact you don't have to look far to find more because in animals, especially dogs, I've found the sixth sense is far more easily accessed than the sixth sense in humans.

This goes back to what I was saying about children being so much better at accessing their psychic abilities than adults – because of their valve being open. Animals can do it for much the same reason: they haven't been tainted by the restraints of the human, adult world.

Did you know, for example, that there are dogs that can detect seizures before they happen? They are called seizure-alert dogs and they warn people with epilepsy of an oncoming attack minutes before it occurs. Sometimes, hours. Which allows the person enough time to take medication, get to a safe place or call for help.

Anything you read about seizure-alert dogs will tell you that scientists have no idea how the dogs detect an oncoming seizure in a human. Trainers and researchers hypothesized that they must detect some change before an episode occurs. However, no scientific studies have proved this theory. Nor is it restricted to a single type of dog. It is simply the case that some dogs are born with this remarkable ability.

Of course, you know what I'm going to say, don't you?

Exactly. The reason scientists have no explanation for this incredible ability is because there is no scientific explanation. It is to do with the dogs' sixth sense. I guess what I'm saying is that dogs are psychic.

Overall, in fact, animals are a very, very interesting case. Not only can they sense spirit world much more keenly than us humans, they exist in spirit world, too.

Thus I'm often asked whether pets join their owners in spirit.

The answer is that it depends on the connection between owner and pet on earth plane.

We have all heard the story about how the ghosts of Roman soldiers are often seen with their horses and I think that is a perfect example of an almost symbiotic bond between animal and owner which carries on in the afterlife.

Same with domestic pets, in my view. John and I had a Jack Russell once, called Holly. We have had a few Jack Russells over the years and I'm going to see them all when I pass over, because we loved them all, but Holly was slightly special, and I know without doubt Holly will be there to greet me first.

Holly went missing. The day after she had gone missing, I was in bed. She always used to sleep with us, just on top of the sheet (this was in the days before duvets). That morning I woke up and Holly was there, asleep on the sheet. As I looked at her, she got to her feet, then leapt towards me. Instinctively, I covered my face with my hands. Holly went straight through me.

I knew, right there and then, that Holly was dead.

John would tell you. I was absolutely devastated, inconsolable. I knew that I had seen Holly in spirit.

Sure enough, a day later Holly was found. She had been run over. Well, I felt the pain of that loss as acutely as anything I have ever felt. Definitely, I mourned for that dog. That is how I know that Holly will be there to greet me when I pass over, because that bond between us was so great.

I'm going to have an awful lot to do, aren't I, when I get there?

Now, still on the subject of dogs, I'll never forget a reading I was doing on stage one night.

This particular reading was for a woman in the front row, which is quite unusual in itself. Don't ask me why, it just is. People often think that if they get front-row seats they are guaranteed a reading, but that is definitely not the case. In fact, I would say that readings tend to take place on those rows slightly further back. I don't know why, I think perhaps it might be something to do with me. But this was unusual, as I say; the woman was in the front row. I was giving her a reading, when all of a sudden I heard a ball bounce and I genuinely thought that somebody had thrown a ball on to the stage.

'Did you hear that?' I said to the woman.

'Yes,' she said.

'Well, I've got the ball here, it rolled over there . . .'

'That's my dog,' she said.

'Is it called Marsh Mellow?' I said, the name just coming to me.

And that was it – her dog, which actually turned out to be called Marshmallow, was on stage with me.

And you'll never guess what happened next! The little rascal stood right next to me and cocked his leg.

A spirit wee!

At that, the woman said, 'That's exactly what Marshmallow used to do.'

Now, I'm always talking about how spirit world will give me details – even gruesome, grisly details of a murder – or unique characteristics to identify themselves to those on earth plane, but without doubt this was the first time that a spirit had weed on me for the purposes of validation.

Shortly after that, there was another show where I found myself saying a name, which was Rafi, or something similar. It was a very unusual one. It can be very difficult sometimes, with the more unusual names. Suddenly, a woman in the audience shouted out, 'Me!'

Just as I got the name Raphael.

'Great, let's get the microphone to you,' I said, and she was given the Cornetto, which is what I call the microphone, by a member of the crew.

'Who's Raphael?' I said, half-expecting it to be her late husband or a parent. I had a man on stage with me, you see.

But no . . .

'Raphael was my cat,' said the woman.

That took me aback, I can tell you.

'Well, darling,' I said, 'I've got a man on stage with me. Either you've got a very big cat or I don't know what.'

As you can imagine, the audience was having a right laugh, but in actual fact it turned out to be one of those cases where an animal was up on stage with other relatives, and when I described the man up on stage with me, he turned out to be a relative of the woman in the audience. The two had found each other in the afterlife.

That was his message for the lady in the audience. He simply wanted to reassure her that Raphael was with him and that Raphael was safe.

Another time, I actually got a grey horse on stage.

I said its name, 'Missy,' and a woman in the audience screamed. Turned out to be her horse.

And the funny thing is, animals do not differ from humans in spirit, so it's not actually inconceivable that I would mistake a dog for a person or vice versa.

Remember, I receive spirits as thoughts in my head, so it is not as if I actually have dogs barking at me. Instead, I have their messages given to me as thoughts. Just the other day, I did a show and was calling out the name Barker.

'Barker, I've got the name Barker, can anybody take a message for somebody with a surname Barker?'

Nobody could, I was having one of my 'erk' moments,

and had begun to wonder if perhaps Barker formed a part of an address, when, suddenly, there was a hand raised at the back.

Barker, it turned out, was the name of a dog.

The dog had passed over and just wanted to make contact with its owner.

Another time, I had the spirit of a cat on stage and gave its name. Once again, a hand was raised in the audience and I located the owner of the cat.

'When did she pass over, then?' I asked.

'Well, we didn't know she had died,' came the answer. 'She went missing about two weeks ago.'

That brought a little bit of a laugh from the audience. And I suppose, if I'm honest, it was slightly funny. At least that was one way to end the mystery of what happened to their moggy.

Thirty-eight

Children and the valve

To cats and dogs, their sixth sense is very much a part of them. It is like another limb; they're incredibly well-developed psychics. It's the same with children, and in my experience, animals and children will often experience spirit phenomena at exactly the same time.

I do signings after my show and one night I saw a lady who said, 'I'd like to know if my dog is psychic.'

I said, 'Well, I can tell you, your dog is psychic, because all animals use their sixth sense, it's a major sense to them. Like our smell and touch and taste, animals have an extra one.'

'Well, Sally,' she went on, 'my grandfather died and my little boy said he saw this man sitting on the end of the sofa, and he described my grandfather. My little boy didn't see him a lot, but I grew up with him so I knew him really well, and it was definitely my grandfather he was describing. I can also smell him around the place. Isn't that funny?'

I shook my head. 'Well, yes and no really, darling. Smell is one of our major indicators of a spirit presence, it really is.'

'There was one particular night, Sally, when my little

boy shouted, "That man's here again on the landing." Then, just at that moment, the dog ran in, came and sat by my feet, looked up at the ceiling, towards where the landing was and began growling. The dog was in the kitchen, so he wasn't upstairs with my little boy in the bedroom, but as soon as my little boy screamed the dog ran in and was growling, and I know he was looking at my grandfather.'

So you can see what was happening there, can't you? The little boy was seeing a spirit, and that dog was sensing him too.

There, in a nutshell, you have a demonstration of everything I've been talking about as regards the valve and the sixth sense, that in adults has been suppressed; you see it working best with pets and youngsters because they haven't yet had their valves closed – or, in the case of animals, never will.

They say, don't they, never work with children or animals? Well, if you're a psychic, that's exactly what you should do, of course.

Here's another example. There are occasions, aren't there, when children have an invisible friend? I get many, many parents who come to me worried about this very thing.

This, often, is put down to some kind of family trauma or loneliness, or there could be other psychological reasons. And that may be so, but I also think there are many children who have invisible friends originating from spirit world. I'll tell you one thing you can almost guarantee: every imaginary friend has the most incredible name. I've heard some right corkers in my time. Where do the kids get these names from? Well, I would say they get their names from a spirit.

The other night somebody came to a show and she told me about her little boy who wakes up screaming, describing a woman in a hat.

'He's five years old,' she said to me. 'He wouldn't know that in the old days you wore bonnets with ribbons, the way he was saying. Yet he had described this woman to a tee, standing there in a long white dress with a big hat on, decorated with a big, pink ribbon.'

In other words, her little boy had accurately described a woman dressed in period costume, and the mother was adamant that, what with him being so young, he simply had no experience of seeing anybody dressed in this manner.

Yet he was seeing her in his bedroom, wandering around at night when he was in bed. Unsurprisingly, this lady wanted to know what was wrong.

There you have it, you see. She wanted to know what was 'wrong'. But why should anything be wrong?

I said, 'No, I don't believe he is going mad. What I think is that your son is psychic – or at least slightly psychic – and he really is seeing this woman.'

'What makes you say that?' she said. 'Is it because of the costume? Because of the clothes she's wearing?'

'Well, that's got something to do with it,' I said, 'but, do you know, it is more to do with what's in my head. I just know – just by looking at you – that your boy is psychic.'

Believe you me, I don't say this to everybody. I get a

lot of parents who come to me and say, 'I think my daughter might be psychic because she sees such-and-such,' or, 'I think my little boy might have psychic ability because he is always talking about so-and-so.'

But very rarely do I ever feel that the children actually have any kind of psychic ability. More often than not it's simply the case that their valves are open, they're uncorrupted, they hit a strong psychic pocket and *whoosh*, they have an afterlife experience.

In this particular instance, though, I just knew that her little boy was psychic.

That leaves me with another dilemma. After all, if I meet someone in the queue at a show, I don't know them from Adam, do I? And the last thing I want is them going home and filling their child's head with nonsense. Kids can easily be manipulated, that's the thing. Their valves are open, so they're naturally quite vulnerable.

My advice, if you feel that your child is displaying some kind of psychic talent – and this would be seeing spirits, invisible friends and so on, and not just once, *but on a regular basis* – is to tread very, very carefully and make sure you don't go too far in either direction.

What I am saying here is, you should really let nature take its course rather than try to impose any of your views or values on your child. After all, you don't want to go opening up the valve on your child too far if it is going to subject them to frightening experiences they are not capable of understanding, do you?

On the other hand, do you want to suppress it? At the end of the day my advice is to play it safe. Keep an open mind, I say – but not so open that your brains fall out.

Thirty-nine

Seeing the signs

Let's imagine you walked into your bedroom and you saw somebody sitting on your bed, and they were solid. I'm not talking see-through or ghostly-looking, but solid, three-dimensional, like you could reach out and take their hand. You do a double-take and they're gone.

What would you think?

I bet you'd assume you'd imagined it, and maybe you did. But what if it happened again? Would you think, 'I've seen a ghost'? Or would you think, 'I need to go and see a doctor'? Let's say it's an old lady you see, because you're more likely to have female ghosts in your house than male ones. (Don't ask me why, but you are.) Later on that evening, you say to your partner, 'Did you leave the bathroom tap running?'

'No,' comes the answer.

You think, 'That's funny. Who left the bloody tap running?'

The next day you and your partner are sitting in your front room and you hear someone in the kitchen. You decide not to mention it to your partner, who turns to you and says, 'Did you just hear something in the kitchen?'

What are the two of you thinking? 'We're both going

round the twist here. We need to see a doctor right away.'

Or are you thinking, 'We have a ghost in our house'?

I truly believe that ninety-nine per cent of people would decide they had a ghost before they assumed that there was something wrong with them. What I am saying is that at some deep, very fundamental level we all, actually, believe in spirits.

One of the questions I'm most frequently asked is: *How can I develop my own ability?*

For a start, the first thing I would say is, ask yourself why you want to do that. If it's because you want to make money, then stop, please – and forget about it.

I never, ever thought, 'I want to be a medium because I can charge people money.' Even when I did eventually begin taking money, I could only really ask £5 a reading. I wouldn't have dreamt of asking for more. When I first started, there were no such things as celebrities. You were a star if you'd made a film or recorded an album. That was it. So it's not like I went into it for that reason either – and let's face it, I'm not exactly your typical celebrity anyway.

So, please, *please* examine your reasons for wanting to do this. If it's money or fame, then forget it.

Second, do you have any actual ability? Or – since I've said that I believe we all have some psychic ability – do you have *enough* ability?

A lot of people get gut feelings and sense things. This is the sixth sense at work. But it's working at a very, very low level. You know those times when you walk into a house that might be a bit dark, a bit cold, and you think, 'I bet there's a ghost in here.' A lot of people take a feeling like that as proof of psychic ability.

Is it? Well, to be honest, not really. Rather, it's evidence that the valve is slightly open. You have the potential, and if you do have feelings like that, you should definitely consider joining a spiritualists' circle. You should also start to look for patterns in your life, clues stretching right back to your childhood.

But as to actual psychic ability? Well, I think it's a situation you should monitor, certainly, but don't put an advert in the *Yellow Pages* just yet.

The people I'm more interested in helping – who I think probably have more potential – are those who say to me, 'Look, I have this precognitive sense to me and I am interested in seeing if I could develop that.' I'm drawn more to these people than those who say, 'I sensed a ghost once. I think I'm going to be a medium,' or those people who – God forbid – come up to me and start telling me they've been talking to Princess Diana. (Yes, unfortunately, my business attracts more than its fair share of complete crackpots.)

The reason for this is that the person who claims to have seen a ghost is usually talking about a one-off incident (the person who says they've spoken to Princess Diana is living in cloud cuckoo land; she's with the princes, darling, believe you me), while those who say they sense things about to happen tend to be describing something they live with day in, day out – and probably have ever since they were a very small child.

Psychic ability can come in different areas. It can be

cognitive premonition. It can be sensing a spirit presence, then having that presence confirmed to you.

I was quite lucky, because I never really had to gather facts. Again, this was as a result of living at Waldemar Avenue. When I moved into a house with John in Orbain Road, London, I knew straight away that it was haunted. But if I hadn't had all those things happen to me as a child, I would have been scurrying around wanting to know what was going on. In a way, I suppose I was a bit blasé having lived at Waldemar. I already had all that evidence and experience. I was able to see the signs.

Normally at the end of the show I wrap up with a little bit of a talk. I thank everyone for being there and I apologize to anyone who hasn't received a message.

I wish I could go to everybody who comes, I really do, but two hours fly by, so I always end up by saying that I would have loved to have given everyone a reading, but that it's impossible. What they have seen is a demonstration.

'You've been a wonderful audience and we've seen some wonder moments' – that's what I call them, my wonder moments – 'and I hope that everybody goes away believing in the incredible, miraculous potential of spirit world.'

What I tell them is to watch out for the signs. I'll say, 'Look for the curtains blowing in the wind when there is no door open and no draught. Be aware of spooky coincidences, like when you turn the radio on and it's a piece of music that both of you loved. Heed your sense of smell and your hearing ...'

That's what I always say to them, though obviously time forbids me from going into as much detail I'd like. So what I'd like to do now, is go into the signs in a little bit more depth.

Forty

Sensual spirit

So much of what I do involves being open to the signs I am given, and this means listening to clues.

What are they? Listen, watch, hear, touch, smell – you'll see them. They're all around us; it's just a case of knowing what to look out for.

At a show not long ago, I had a man in spirit who wanted to tell his wife that he was moving the mat. This lady in the audience was absolutely amazed. You could tell that suddenly things were making sense to her.

'I told my son that the mat keeps moving,' she said, laughing.

'That mat is your sign, darling,' I explained to her. For whatever reason, her hubby in spirit was moving the mat. It was his way of saying, 'Here I am. I'm still with you, darling.'

I dare say she wouldn't have seen it as a sign beforehand; it was coming to me that unlocked it for her, if you like. However, it's exactly that kind of thing you should be looking out for.

Other signs? Well, I always say to look out for the senses. Spirit world can really affect the senses – all *six* of them.

Take smell, for example. If somebody passed over who

always smoked a certain brand of cigars, for instance, or a woman who always wore a particular perfume, their loved ones would, at some point, smell that particular smell.

When I die – I'm sure of this – one of my family will smell me. And, no, not the way you're thinking! They will smell my perfume, and it is a particular brand of perfume that I always wear, so I know they will smell it and they'll think of me. I don't mean they're going to go into Boots and smell my perfume, but they will be somewhere quite random when, for some reason unknown to them, that perfume smell will come to them. That'll be me, in spirit, triggering that sense, reminding them of me.

When I'm away, my John says that he can smell my perfume, and it's in a particular room of the house in which I very, very rarely sit. So, not only is there no chance whatsoever that traces of my perfume will be on the furniture, but he only ever smells the scent when I am away.

Now, obviously, I'm alive. Even so, I am triggering his sixth sense.

I saw a lady a while back who was telling me about the smell of cigar smoke in her house.

The rest of the family agreed they could smell *something*, and that it did smell a lot like smoke ... But they refused to believe it could be cigar smoke. This was for the simple reason that nobody had smoked in the house. Therefore, they refused to believe they could smell cigar smoke.

However, this lady was convinced that the smell of cigar smoke had something to do with her late father.

Speaking to her, it turned out that every Sunday her

father had used to enjoy a cigar after lunch. And wouldn't you know it? Remember everything I've said about how spirit can seem particularly active on the anniversary of a death? Well, this smell of cigar smoke had appeared around that time.

There you have it. A smell. One of the most common ways for spirit to manifest itself. I tell everyone this – anyone who'll listen. You really need to pay attention to that sense; it is absolutely key to an understanding of spirit. I've lost count of the times I've had a smell – of perfume, of smoke, of sweaty armpits, even. That sense means so much to spirit, it really does.

This leads me on to taste. A lot of people find they have a sensation of taste following that of smell. This is, obviously, because the two senses are so close together. I find that if somebody has died quite a violent death, what I get is a very strong, salty taste in my mouth, which I think is the taste of blood.

Listen out for things, too.

I spoke to a woman the other day who was telling me about strange noises she heard in her house.

'It can be really quiet during the day and I hear a noise, but I know no one is there. There are times when I hear the front door, though, and I think the postman is knocking or something, but there's no post and nobody has been up or down the drive. What do you think it is, Sally?'

'Who did you recently lose?' I asked her. 'Who are you grieving?'

'This is the thing, Sally,' she said, 'no one. Not … recently.'

'But there is someone, isn't there?' I said. 'Who is that? Who have you lost?'

'My husband,' she said. 'He died two years ago.'

OK, I thought.

'Was it about this time of year?' I said carefully.

'Yes, it was,' she confirmed, 'it was this month.'

'Well, that's it then. There's always a lot of spirit activity around a certain date. It's being triggered by you, because you are either consciously or subconsciously thinking about your husband as it is the anniversary of his death. Because he is on your mind at some hidden level you are inviting the spirit in and he is just reminding you of himself. He's just saying, "Hello, I'm here."'

'Do you think?'

'I'm sure of it, darling, absolutely sure of it.'

Now, you might think that she needed me to bring her comfort, needed a medium to help decode the signals being given to her by spirit world. But this is my point. I think you can decode the signal yourself if you are open to doing so. Most people, you see, if they hear a noise, will disregard it or put it down to something else. What I'm saying is, don't discount that noise out of hand.

Another sign to look out for is touch. Have you ever felt a touch and there's been no one touching you?

If so, then I strongly suggest you were being visited by a spirit. One place to be very aware of this is the bed, for some reason.

Spirits sit on our beds a lot. I know, it sounds mad, doesn't it? But they do. People often wake up and can see people sitting on the bed next to them. Then, when they pull the covers over themselves, the spirit is still there, unmoved, undisturbed.

I myself have had experiences of spirits sitting on the end of my bed and trapping my feet. This is quite rare, to have touch and sight together like this, but it's worth looking out for.

Also, look out for coincidences. Telepathy, for example. I find this is most common in couples. You may have found it yourself. Perhaps you and your other half have the same thought at the same time. To me, that's evidence of telepathy at work. Most people would not see it as evidence of our sixth sense though, so it tends to go unnoticed, unremarked and, therefore, undeveloped.

This is an extension of my point before, that because there are so many of us who don't believe in sixth sense it has lain dormant.

Something else that you should keep an eye out for are those animals acting as representatives of spirit on earth plane. Birds, in particular.

One night on tour, I had the name 'Bessy', which I called out, and the microphone went to a lady in the audience.

Immediately, I felt a pain in my chest.

'What's that pain here, I can feel?' I asked her.

She swallowed. 'My mum died suddenly. She died of DVT.'

'Oh my God, and it travelled to her lung?'

'Yes.'

'That's why – that's why I can feel the pain here. And the name Bessy?'

'That's me, that's my name.'

Now I could see a place, a bungalow, and told her so.

'Where am I?' I asked her. 'What am I seeing? It's a bungalow.'

'Yes,' said Bessy, 'that's where she died.'

I go there, said the spirit. I could feel the thought introducing itself into my head. I don't think I'll ever be able to find the words to adequately express how spirit appears in my head.

I go back to the bungalow, said the spirit.

'Are there still people living in that bungalow?' I asked now.

'My dad still lives there,' she said.

I received other thoughts. Some garbled and indistinct; some not. Then, clear as a bell, came a thought about the washing.

'The washing?' I repeated. 'She's not happy about the washing. She's worried about the washing.'

I sensed this concern in spirit. But even as the lady in the audience assimilated this latest message, something new came to me.

'If I said to you robin, a little robin bird, would you know what I meant?'

There are times – times like then, in fact – when I throw out something completely random like 'if I said to you robin' and I really wonder where we're going with it. You've heard about performers 'flying by the seat of their pants'? Try being a psychic on stage.

'Yes,' she said, 'yes.'

At least she knew what I meant by the robin.

'What's that?'

'When Mum passed away, a little robin appeared,' she

said. 'And every so often my sister gets a little robin in the garden.'

'That's your sign, darling,' I said, pointing towards her, knowing exactly that was what it was. Her mother was still visiting her, and she was appearing as a robin. I knew it as surely as I knew my own name. Robins often are signs, actually; one of those animals that is particularly symbolic.

Then, of course, you have your sixth sense. And if we are talking about looking out for the signs then, whatever you do, do not ignore the sixth sense.

This is the sense that will give you the 'feeling' that somebody is with you in spirit. Like when you are alone and you get the sense that somebody is in the room with you and you turn around only to find nobody is there. That's your sixth sense talking.

Now, I can talk about these signs until I'm blue in the face, I really can. I can talk about smells and dogs and moving doormats and robins until the cows come home. But the question that most frequently arises is, *When?*

When is my loved one going to make himself or herself apparent?

Brace yourself for another one of Sally Morgan's famous theories.

I'm going to tell you all about the cling-film effect.

Forty-one

The cling-film effect

Something that I talk about a lot of the time when I'm discussing bereavement is the cling-film effect.

Bereavement, I truly believe, knocks us off our axis. There we are, padding along, quite happy. Then, we lose a loved one. To the brain, this amazing computer we are blessed with, it is just like that amazing computer crashing. *Bang.* In a way, we sort of implode.

And what we do is, we wrap ourselves in bereavement, a bit like – wait for it – cling film.

I believe that this is because if we actually knew the enormity of death, of bereavement, we really would implode, shut down, cease to function. If you have ever had the death of someone close to you, then I'm sure you'll know what I mean. There are times when it feels as though you're simply going to be swallowed up whole by the darkness.

So bereavement acts as a shield, in a way. The cling film wraps itself around us; it actually protects us, believe it or not. You could say that it is protecting us from exploding, from melting down.

And as time goes by – it could be a week, a month, a year, or longer – that cling film rolls down. It exposes us once again, but only when we're ready for it.

Now, what I think is that the cling film, when it's protecting you, keeps you safe not only from grief, but from all other interference. Literally nothing can get through, even spirit. But eventually the cling film starts to come off. And as soon as that happens, those people who have had difficulty in sensing their loved ones before can begin to feel them.

They couldn't before, you see? They were too wrapped up in that cling film. The very same cling film that was protecting them.

An example of this happened just the other day, at a show. A lady I spoke to – well, you could see she simply didn't believe that her husband, in spirit, was making contact with her.

Why had it taken him so long, was what she wanted to know.

I attempted to explain that I believe contact is generated by the spirit of their loved one in the afterlife, and that it comes at a time that corresponds to the anniversary of their death.

She said to me, 'But, that can't be, Sally. He died two years ago and I've never felt his presence. I've never had these signs you're talking about. Nothing, not a word.'

'He's with you, darling,' I said.

This was in the queue, but I could feel he was with her there. Officially, I'm closed when I'm doing signings, but between you and me, I'm still picking up stuff.

'Well, then . . .' you could see her struggling with the words, 'why has it taken him so long?'

I explained to her about the cling-film effect. That it was her grief wrapping itself around her, protecting her, then – when the job was done, when the cling film began to peel away – only then would she able to feel the presence of her husband in the afterlife.

It makes perfect sense if you think about it. After all, we all react differently to different things. So when you look at bereavement, the only common denominator is the fact that we have lost someone. Apart from that, yes, there are symptoms that we will all experience, but the intensity and the exact nature of those symptoms will vary from person to person.

For every person who comes to me saying that it's taken two years before they start smelling cigar smoke on a Sunday afternoon, there will be somebody else come to me saying that they felt the presence of their husband just an hour after his funeral.

Or even *at* his funeral: 'I felt him there,' is such a common thing for me to hear.

But it's because one is not covered in cling film, the other one is.

Now, the thing is that lots of people who come to me wearing the cling film don't want it there. They want to feel that their loved one is around them, especially if they have recently been bereaved, which I suppose is the most likely reason they come to my door in the first place.

Once I have explained the cling film, more often than not they'll say, 'Well, how do I get rid of this cling film, then?' They don't want it there, of course.

What I need to do at times like that is explain to them that though they may not *want* it there, they certainly *need* it there. It's like people who have to take blood pressure tablets. They don't want to take them, but they have to because they don't want to pop a gasket. Then there are people who are exactly the same weight and age, everything else, who have never needed a blood pressure tablet in their lives.

The fact is that bereavement affects some more than others. Me, I get through my door all different kinds of people experiencing bereavement in all different ways.

Yes, possibly the most common type are those who come in shock, really; those who are still experiencing the sudden jolt of losing a loved one. But I have a couple of women, who are a similar age to me, who lost their husbands years ago, who perfectly illustrate what I'm talking about.

One is an Italian lady, who always comes dressed from head to toe in black, still mourning, like Queen Victoria.

Another lady, who is English, is also, I would say, still coming to terms with her husband's death.

Both of those women's husbands died about seven or eight years ago. And it might as well have happened that day. They're in shock. They still cannot talk about their husbands without crying. They carry photographs. They come with their daughters, both of them do, and over the years I've watched the daughters change: the daughters no longer cry, but the mothers still do.

On the other hand, I have women who come to me who are grieving and who really miss their husbands, but don't shed a tear. They just sit there, their hands in their laps, looking very stoical.

These people come to see me for many reasons, but mainly because they want to know that their loved ones are OK and in spirit world. In other words, what they want to know is, *is there an afterlife?* And if their loved one is all right. Are they safe? They're not lost, are they? They're not on their own?

I have seen thousands upon thousands of people and I would say that every single one of them is just desperate to know that the light hasn't gone out on their loved one; that their loved one hasn't just vanished.

The two ladies who still come to see me years after the passing of their other halves are the same as any other clients; the same as anyone who comes to see me at one of my shows. They want reassurance that their loved one is there in spirit world, happy, safe, watching over them.

The only way they can truly be reassured that this is the case is by speaking to the spirit of their loved one – which they can only do through me. They may have signs in their daily life – the smells, the sixth sense we've been talking about – but if they are anything like ninety-nine per cent of people they will still need that confirmation they can only get from talking to somebody like me.

As you know, I do that by talking to the spirit of their loved one and giving information to the person on earth plane – that validation I'm always on about.

To validate something you have to be accurate. So I have to give them something that there's no way I could know.

Sometimes it strikes me what an enormous responsibility it is; what a pressure there is on my shoulders to make things right for those who sit opposite me, whether it's in my office or at one of my shows.

I'm giving them a huge amount of comfort. But if I get

it wrong and spirit world gives me garbled messages, or even the wrong message, then I could easily shake a person's faith, not only in the ultimate fate of their loved one, but in spirituality itself.

And the thing is, I need to do this every time I speak to somebody. Those two ladies who visit may have lost their husbands years and years ago, but when I speak to them for the first time and give them validation that they're talking to the right spirit, that doesn't then absolve me from having to do it next time I speak to them.

In short, each of them needs validation every time they come. I mean, if I saw one of them on Monday, her reading would be different on a Tuesday, because it's a different day, but she still wants that validation. Each time she comes she still wants to know that her husband's in heaven. And he is – he's still there. He hasn't gone anywhere. I tell her each time she comes, 'He's still around you, and you are still here, so he is still here.'

She goes away happy.

Then, of course, I get people who come to me wanting to know specific things from those who have passed. It's funny, I get a lot of people who want to know where to find things. Recently, at a show, I had a woman who was sitting in the front of the audience and I had her husband in spirit on stage with me.

I said, 'Oh, your husband is saying to me, where is his chain?'

She looked at me. She was standing up. She said, 'Chain?'

I said, 'Yeah, he wore a chain. What have you done with it?'

'All that went missing when he was still alive,' she said.

'It's in his fishing box,' I said.

She looked at me, open-mouthed. 'How did you know he went fishing?' she said.

'Well, he's got a fishing box,' I said. 'It's in that.'

Sure enough . . .

Forty-two

Contacting the other side

So, let's talk about contacting the other side.

I always say that a thought is a prayer. I mean, it's not a case of, 'Let's just call up.' If you really are serious about it, it helps to sit quietly and contemplate and that's another way we can reach spirit – we can send a thought out to them.

Let me give you an example of that from a show I did and, oh my goodness, it was one of those readings that I thought was going to fall completely flat, because I just kept getting no, no, *no*.

This happens so much during a show and I always need to stop and remind people that it really is up to them to interpret the messages because I am not capable of doing so. Here's a perfect example of that in action.

It was at one of my 'psychic cam' features, where I invite people to leave a little video message. One of them was a young girl, very pretty, who said, 'I want some kind of communication with my mum who passed away five years ago. I want to know if she's here tonight and if she has anything to say to me.'

I immediately felt as though I had her mother in spirit. Plus, I had a very strong impression of curtains. In fact, what I could see was a bed, with a curtain across it.

'Where you sleep,' I said, 'do you sleep in a bed with curtains, like a four-poster bed?'

She'd been given the microphone and she held it to her mouth now. A camera goes on to the person in the audience, so everybody could see her raise the microphone to her mouth, and say . . .

'No.'

The worst word for someone in my job.

Still, though, I pressed on. I tell you, I have no choice in a situation like that. I just have to trust and push on.

'I feel like I'm in your bedroom,' I said. 'This is going to sound mad, OK, because we all have curtains and windows, but I feel as if I'm near a bed . . .'

She was looking at me blankly. The night had been going so well, too. Message after message after message. They're not all like that, but this one had been going brilliantly.

Until now.

'Do your curtains hang on your bed?' I asked her.

'No,' she said, shaking her head.

A lot of the time I simply come to the conclusion that I'm reading for the wrong person, and I'll try to follow the path of what I call a 'psychic thermal', but there was something about this one . . . Even though she was shaking her head, I was *sure* I had something here.

So, doggedly, I ploughed on.

'Do the curtains blow on your bed?' I tried . . .

'No,' she said. She was shaking her head now and looking a little embarrassed. 'I haven't got curtains,' she added.

'I'm with your mum,' I said, still pressing forward. I

was sure about this, I really was, 'and I'm in a bedroom and there are curtains, and it's like they can fall on the bed and it's as if I want to push them off the bed . . .'

'No,' she said, shaking her head.

Still I persisted. 'Have you stayed anywhere recently? It was a special occasion or something to remember? And it was very special. Your mum was with you?'

And suddenly it clicked. She went from shaking her head and looking somewhat embarrassed to getting it.

'Oh,' she gasped, 'I know what you're talking about . . .'

'Go on . . .'

'I recently . . .' she started.

But that was as far she could go. For then she was breaking down, crying.

'Mummy was there, darling,' I assured her.

She gathered herself together: 'I went to buy some curtains for my front room,' she said, 'and when I was in the shop I remembered that the last time I went to buy curtains I had to ring her to ask what size I needed, so when I got to the shop I really thought *I need my mum* . . .'

She broke down.

'She was there, darling,' I told her. 'She knew. Do you know what? A thought is a prayer. Every time you think of your mother, it's like sending out a little prayer to her. Were there beds in the shop, darling?'

'Yes, there were,' she confirmed.

She was showing me a double bed.

Wow. It was quite a reading. For a start I had to play the trust game. I had to believe that spirit was being straight with me, even though the girl was saying, 'No,' and looking a little uncomfortable and people in the audience were getting a bit restless. Nervous moments, I can tell you.

But then it clicked, which was a lesson to me not to let my trust waver. And it ended up being a perfect illustration of the way that spirits look out for us in the afterlife; how, when we reach out towards them, they're listening, even if it feels that sometimes they're not.

Sending out that thought – merely thinking of the person – can often be all it takes to summon your spirits. Also, believe it or not, you can just quietly talk to them. A lot of people are surprised when I tell them that.

I had a lady the other day who was telling me about a ghost in her house that was freaking her out a little.

'What can I do about it, Sally?' she asked me.

'You know, darling, one thing you can do is just talk to it.'

'You're joking?'

'No – if you're frightened just say, "Go away, I don't want you here. You're frightening me."'

'Really?'

'Yes, really. Most of the time simply telling the spirit to go away will work. It's as easy as that. People think because it's the unknown or the unseen and because it's to do with dead people that somehow there has to be some kind of hocus pocus involved in it, but of course there isn't. I talk to spirits – spirits can hear us here on earth plane – so why on earth can't you just speak to a ghost and order it to go away? You know those cases you hear about when an exorcism is needed, or some-one goes in and tries to get rid of the ghost? They are those instances where a ghost has refused to heed the command of the home-owner.'

This particular lady went away and, sure enough, it worked, her telling the spirit to leave the house. That was a weird situation, because the spirit presumably knew the family were frightened by its activity. Perhaps it took them articulating that out loud to convince the spirit to leave. Perhaps it was the case that as soon as it knew the family were on to it, then the fun was over.

I would like to feel that throughout this book I have tried to demystify the process of listening to spirits, and I would like to do the same with the process of talking to them. So, on that note, let's talk about Ouija boards.

Horrible things, if you ask me.

Normally, Ouija boards are used by people who are not mediums and they're used just for a laugh.

Listen, there's nothing wrong in having a laugh with spirit, I do it every night on stage, but you have to know what you're doing. And most people who use Ouija boards simply don't know what they're doing. Yes, you can use them to contact spirits – I won't lie about that. But don't. That's my advice to you – to anybody who asks me.

You'll summon a spirit that you shouldn't. You know me, I call up spirit when somebody comes to me wanting to contact their relatives and I have a certain amount of control during that process. But if you have a Ouija board, you can get mischievous spirits appearing who will say things that you do not want to hear. They will do things you do not want. You know how they say that if you listen at a door you will hear something about your-self that you shouldn't be hearing? It's the same with a Ouija board. Ugh. I do think they're horrible things.

No, the only way other than actually speaking I would suggest you try to contact spirit is by automatic writing.

To do that you must sit there, relaxing, either watching television or listening to music with a pen in your hand and a piece of paper. After a while the pen will just move. This is something most people can try. In fact, I think it is sometimes the first introduction people have who want to know a little bit about spirit. You just literally hold a pen and take a piece of paper, relax, don't think of anything and it will move and write.

When I was in America, I did this for somebody whose friend had died in a car accident, and I wrote 'gotcha' twice on a piece of paper. It turned out that 'gotcha' related to a game the two friends used to play. This guy literally could not believe it, because before I started he was a total sceptic and non-believer.

It began when he showed me a picture of himself with some college friends and I pointed out one man in particular and I said, without knowing a thing about the people in the picture, 'This man is in spirit; he was decapitated.'

The guy looked at me and said, 'What did you just say?'

'He lost his head,' I said. 'It was cut off in ... a car accident?'

It had come to me in an instant.

Before you knew it, we were doing some automatic writing, and what came from that was the word 'gotcha'. Now, this really blew the guy's mind; it freaked him out and he ended the meeting singing the Monkees' song, 'I'm a Believer'.

It's something I had done many times before and have done many times since.

The trick is to relax and hardly even hold the pen. The last thing you want to be doing is moving the pen because it really is a case of letting spirit move it for you. So if you do try it, don't be tempted to surreptitiously move the pen yourself.

As is always the case with any of your dealings with the afterlife, you have to be guided by spirit.

Forty-three

Thoughts and worries . . .

I have a lot of people who say to me, especially after shows, 'Why is it that the messages from the afterlife are always so positive?'

It makes me laugh that question, because it's right. I never get, 'He hates your guts and still doesn't forgive you for what you did to his fish.'

Almost always the message from the other side is one of reassurance and comfort.

To those who ask, I always say that my job is as a medium, to provide a gateway between this world and the afterlife. Those opportunities come very rarely, both for those of us on earth plane and those in the spirit world.

Spirits are, in the main, over the moon to make contact with their loved ones on earth plane. It's a bit like when you're watching one of those Saturday night TV shows that reunites a family, half of whom have moved to Australia: there's a family in the studio in the UK, then they link to another part of the family in Australia, standing on a beach, waving and smiling, saying what a great time they're having. They don't stand there scowling and complaining about something that happened five years ago. They don't start a family row, do they?

No, of course not. The fact is, they're just chuffed to

see each other. It is a lot like that when it comes to messages from spirit world. That, plus the fact that spirit are, in the main, happier on the other side and don't waste time whinging and bitching and moaning. What would be the point of that?

And, of course, they always come. It's funny, because one of my big worries doing the show was, believe it or not, that the spirits simply would not turn up.

I still get it now. Every night, I'm having a baby at the side of the stage. I say to Julie, the production manager's wife, 'Oh my God, I feel like I'm having a baby, my tummy's going over, I'm all out of breath.'

In short, it's excruciating.

But, touch wood (you'll have to imagine me tapping the side of my head here), it has never happened. I don't think I have ever walked on to a stage at any show which has not been packed with spirits.

Obviously, I am open from almost the minute I step on to that stage, and there is like . . . I can only describe it as a clamour. I spend a few minutes just chatting to the audience, warming up, but you can guarantee that there will be one or two very, very insistent spirits who insist on being heard straight away. I have lost count of the amount of times one of my carefully worked intros has been derailed by an over-enthusiastic spirit. Happens all the time, I can tell you. Very often, they provide the best readings of the night.

Even so, the next night, I am at the side of the stage, still having babies, still saying to Julie, 'Oh my God, what if there are no spirits there tonight?'

I think it's because of that doubt thing I was talking

about, the fear that my ability might suddenly disappear. One way I counteract any hesitancy is to think to myself, 'Well, if I'm not meant to do this, something will happen that will stop me from doing it.' You see, I truly believe I was put on earth to do this work. That's why I sort of assume that I will be recycled back down here almost as soon as I pass over.

That's the way I deal with it anyway. I suppose you could say it's rather a fatalistic view. I simply say to myself that I'm doing this because I'm meant to be doing it.

I think that if I am ever given to moments of severe self-doubt, then it is more likely to involve a worry I have that the spirits will not be happy with how I relay their messages – or that those who get messages will not be happy with them.

When I do a show, I have around 2,000 people in the audience every night, and I am worried by the sheer numbers of people involved. The way I get around it is to imagine my front room when I'm standing on stage and I concentrate on patches of about ten people to conquer my nerves. Thinking about this is how I prepare myself prior to going on. I try to visualize these small, manageable sections of people. Then, about five minutes before I go on, I get what they call 'house clearance', which is when the management tell me that the front of house is clear and that all of the audience has taken their seats and no one is left in the bar, at which point they begin playing a film montage which announces my entrance.

And this is when I always think, 'Why am I doing this?'

Forty-four

Why do I do it?

It's the same when I come off at half time. Every night, even if it's been brilliant, I always think to myself, 'Well, that was very average.' And I say to Julia as I'm walking down to my dressing room to change, 'Why *am* I doing this?'

What on earth possesses me? Why would anybody want to put themselves through this every single night? No script, all improvisation, relying on spirit world to give me messages, hoping they will be messages people want to hear. Whenever I go on stage I look at the faces out there and I think, *Oh my God, they are all waiting for little old me to talk.*

So why do it, you wonder? After all, before *Star Psychic* I had a thriving home practice. Because I had been Princess Diana's psychic, I was virtually guaranteed a steady supply of clients. For that same reason, without wanting to sound big-headed, I could charge rather more than the average psychic working from home. So, if I'd wanted to, I could have settled down and continued working from home.

But I chose not to because one of the things I had enjoyed so much about *Star Psychic* was, even more than the challenge, the meeting new people. Of course I get to meet new people in my practice, but it's not quite the same; the opportunities are certainly less varied, let's put it like that. On the TV show, and out on tour, I literally never know what's going to happen next. That keeps me on my toes, I think. It makes me a better, more competent psychic.

If I'm right, and if I was put on earth in order to do this work, then I owe it to him upstairs to do that work to the best of my abilities, to make contact with as many people as possible. And the thing is, the more I have taken the show around and about, and up and down the country, the more that stage has become my comfort zone. And what I return to more than anything, is the fulfillment I get from bringing comfort and closure to those I see. In other words, I want to make people happy. Which is a laugh in itself, because so many of my readings – well, I suppose about ninety per cent of them – end with a person in tears, which isn't really a great way to measure whether or not somebody's happy.

They are, though. I hope I've demonstrated that enough throughout this book – that even the most heart-breaking readings always end with some form of positive resolution for the person I'm reading for.

That's why I say that every reading is like a little miracle. I call them my wonder moments, as I said before, and I think that the day I stop being amazed at what I can do, or at the beauty and intricacies of spirit world, is the day I should stop doing it, really.

As it is, I get too much personal satisfaction, too much pleasure, from doing the work to ever stop.

It's funny, because most readings will touch on areas

that are incredibly moving for the person involved. I'm not a hard person, so I am always affected. Of course, I try my best not to let some of the more emotional readings get to me – I'd go mad with grief if I were to contemplate for too long some of the terrible suffering and sadness that people go through – but I really do go on a journey with that other person and I do think that the effectiveness of my work is not just my ability to sit and communicate with dead people, but also my ability to empathize with and understand those who are left behind on earth plane.

I remember, not long after I had finished filming *Star Psychic*, a woman came to see me at home.

The reading began and I had a lady in spirit that I described to her. It was her mother. She brought out a photograph of her to show me and it was indeed the same woman. For a moment or so, my client seemed pleased that she was in touch with her mother.

'Your mum feels a bit annoyed about where she is,' I told the woman.

Now, if you've got this far in the book, then you will know that this is quite unusual – spirits are usually happy on the other side. That fact gave me pause for thought, but it was nothing compared to the effect it had on my client, who began backtracking all of a sudden.

She said, 'Oh no, that's not my mum.'

I knew it was her mum. At the same time it clicked what the problem was. The woman's mother was feeling frustrated because, for whatever reason – sadly, I never found out why – the woman wasn't letting her in.

'Well, just a minute, listen, darling, your mum is really

annoyed where she is. One of the reasons is that she'd really like to feel she could contact you and talk to you, but she can't. Are you having difficulty feeling her?'

'No,' she said.

But she wasn't being entirely truthful, either with me or with herself.

'OK,' I said uncertainly, not quite sure what was happening here, 'you know your mum better than I do.'

The rest of the reading went along similar lines. Everything I said, she didn't want to know about. It was as though she simply did not want to engage with any of the messages I was being given for her.

In the end she said, 'I don't want this reading to continue.'

I said, 'OK, fair enough. Neither do I, because I don't think you are ready to speak to your mum.'

'You haven't got my mum,' she said. 'My mum wouldn't have been like that. When my mum died, I know that she was really happy to die, because she had been so ill, she was looking forward to the afterlife.'

'I know where you're coming from, darling,' I said, 'but this woman was speaking to me. I'm telling you, she's your mother.'

We reviewed a couple of things that had been said – messages given to me by the woman in spirit. The client agreed that, yes, those messages could only have come from her mother.

'Well,' I said, 'if you agree with those, then why aren't you seeing it? Why can't you accept that this is your mother talking to you in spirit?'

'Because it's not her,' the woman insisted, shaking her head.

And you know what? It just didn't happen. I ended up giving her her money back. The reading had only lasted five minutes and she was clearly unhappy with the outcome. It was only right that she got a refund.

What I love about my job, as I've already said, is helping people by bringing about a comfort and closure into their lives. With this woman, though, I had quite comprehensively failed, it seemed.

Why?

I really beat myself up about it. I wandered around the house in a right old two and eight. Why had things gone so terribly wrong? In all my years, I don't think I'd ever had a reading that had gone quite so badly. I hadn't managed to create a connection, there had been no bond between us at all.

In the end, I think that was the problem. Somehow, for whatever reason, we simply hadn't managed to establish the bond that I need in order to be able to work most effectively.

I put it down to experience. OK, Sally, that was the one that got away. I decided to learn from it and move on. Whatever doesn't kill you makes you stronger and all that.

Shortly afterwards, though, I was talking to Fern, who used to take my bookings. I asked her about this particular reading. It turned out that the woman had phoned up beforehand, wanting to postpone. However, I was going out on tour and not taking future bookings at that time. Fern told as her much, and simply offered to refund her deposit. Rather than take the refund, though, the woman had come along anyway.

Now, that struck me as very interesting. There was obviously a great reluctance on her part. She didn't really want to be in the room. She wasn't happy with the information she had about her mother, and just didn't want to hear what I had to say. Why? I couldn't say. But it just goes to show that when I make contact with spirit world, it's very much a three-person job. Me, the spirit and the sitter. If you get one who is unwilling then, sorry, it just ain't going to work.

Still, I suppose that reading was what they call the exception that proves the rule. Because otherwise I've been incredibly fortunate in being able to create that all-important connection with those I'm reading for.

I really do feel it is one of my great strengths as a medium, and why I have managed to reach a certain level in my field. It's because, well, I think because I have *empathy*. I don't judge, you see. And if you read my last book you will know that I have a few skeletons in my own closet. No way am I squeaky clean. So I never judge those I've read for, whatever they've done.

There you have an instance of how my life has informed my career; I often wonder whether there's been somebody up there, pulling the strings, leading me through a life that better equips me to help others. Maybe the puppet master wanted a certain amount of hardship for me, in order that I should be able to better understand those I read for – so I can more easily create that connection. Either way, I truly believe that my life as a psychic has been a case of gradually preparing me to do the work that I'm doing now.

I'll give you an example. If I had met the belly dancer when I was an eight-year-old girl, do you think I would have been shown the images I was given that afternoon in the studio in Wimbledon?

I don't think so.

I think I was being shown those pictures in the certainty that I would be able to process them – to *deal with them*, if you like.

Yes, I saw shocking things growing up. I saw spirits that were not totally benign. Certainly I was shown more than a young girl my age should really have seen.

As the adult Sally Morgan, though, I see these things all of the time. That poor man running through the trees, only to be beaten to death. That poor little lad who rode his bicycle into the woods to hang himself, just to see what it was like.

No, I am sure that my life has prepared me for my work. It has been a training ground. Just now I said that whatever doesn't kill you makes you stronger. With me, whatever doesn't kill me makes me better. A better medium. Better able to help those who need my help.

And that's why I do it, I guess. It's a caring thing. Throughout my life people have said to me that I should be a therapist or enter psychiatry; for years I worked as a nurse, a job that helped nurture the side of me that just wants to help people; and for my whole life I've been a medium, where, I'm happy to say, I've been able to bring comfort and reassurance to literally thousands of people.

Well, I've had a little help, of course. It's all down to

spirit world, really. Thanks to that moment in 1979 in the South London Hospital for Women, and countless moments since, I know something very profound about spirit world. That it's a place where they blast away all of our earth-plane imperfections to reveal what lies beneath: a light. The most powerful in the universe, the one that guides us, that heals us, the greatest gift we can give. *Love*.